THE EARTH IN THE HEAVENS

Ruling Degrees of Cities, How to Find and Use Them

By

L. Edward Johndro

SAMUEL WEISER INC.

New York

1970

Originally published, 1929

SAMUEL WEISER INC.
734 Broadway
New York, N. Y. 10003

This edition is limited to 750 copies

Standard Book Number: 87728-012-6

Printed in U.S.A. by
NOBLE OFFSET PRINTERS, INC.
NEW YORK 3, N. Y.

CONTENTS

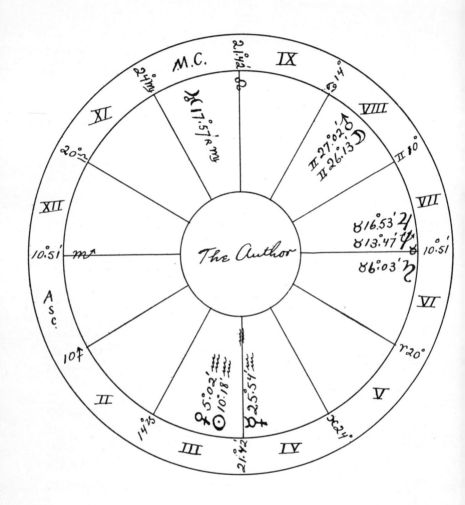

PREFACE

The first intention was to publish the table given in this work and leave the reader to utilize it as his training might dictate. It was seen, however, that to do so would in no adequate degree place the longitudinal co-ordinates on a parity with the latitudinal equations as determinable from the author's work on the fixed stars.

It was next attempted to make the treatment still more simple than in its present form. But it was found that to do this meant the slighting of so many technical considerations that the only result would be to foster in the researcher the hasty conclusion that the given Greenwich base must be sadly amiss; since if arcs are measured only in the ecliptic, or directions are computed by more popular through unwarranted methods, the table would too frequently fail to satisfy the equations, though seeming perhaps to occasionally fit an event.

It was finally decided to sufficiently enlarge the work to include such technicalities as would best give the reader a glimpse of what astrology might become under the guidance of electrical laws, yet leave the beginner free to shirk, in part, these tedious refinements with some understanding why his simpler equations must often fail if he chooses to adhere to them.

More important, perhaps, than that this treatise should be entirely within the grasp of the average astrological student, is the need of encouraging scientific thought on a subject which before the advent of radio was so inexplicable to the average mind as to invite almost universal ridicule.

That under their observations the theory of planetary influence on organic life proved its case to the satisfaction of Kepler, Newton, Bacon and other great minds was for the great majority of men not enough. Heretofore to science the Invisible Power has been something to be sought only near to hand in the test tube or in the biologic cell upon the microscopic slide; to religion something to be blindly worshipped afar from the church pew.

When the alleged "wrath of God" in the form of lightning resolved itself, by the experiments of Franklin, into a natural expression of electrical law under the given conditions, the race, still dumb, grew a little bolder. But with the dynamo, telegraph and telephone came still little but human vanity and a keener desire for further emancipation from a stupid fate. Only with the advent of radio and its attendant explosion of first etheric theories, and only with the coincident breakdown of early atomic concepts as the electronic swarms became better revealed, has conceited man faltered of condemnation of what he does not understand.

Today, in awe, science through thousands of hands and minds knocks more reverentially, less scoffingly, at the very citadel of the Invisible Power; seeking to know its ways; mindful of what the last two decades have brought; eager, yet withal fearful what the next may bring; admitting the structure of the atom to be, in principle, in the image of the solar system seen figuratively, as it were, by the reversion of the telescope into the microscope—the same world through different spectacles fitted to eyes but lately trained to see; viewing time's foreshortening in the ever ascending electrical frequencies with which it ingeniously conjures; acknowledging light waves to be necessary to life and devising relatively low-wave generators as if not curealls at least possible aids to health; witnessing the while the breakdown of dielectrics into conductors and the automatic transformation of conductors into first-class resistances as experiments but distantly approach the frequencies which concern this text; noting the physiological and psychological reactions of its strange devices upon the workers who toil in laboratories toward their perfection.

If amidst all this crumbling of earlier scientific precepts and precedents there still be those who cannot see in our solar system the manifestations of the same electrical laws that bind up the atom and belt the earth with if not the music of the spheres, at least a fair imitation bearing youthful promise, let them hesitate in their ridicule of astrological theory long enough to await the easily predictable verdict of science on Einstein's recent pronouncement that the laws of gravitation and magnetism are one, and to ponder whether, this being so, God's will and love become less supreme and sweet if presently we see:

> They, too, reach out in this one law
> To govern far and near,
> Till man by wisdom shall stand free
> To choose and engineer.

—The Author.

April, 1929,
San Bernardino, Cal.

O how far removed,
Predestination! is thy foot from such
As see not the First Cause entire; and ye,
O mortal men! be wary how ye judge;
For we, who see the Maker, know not yet
The number of the chosen; and esteem
Such scantiness of knowledge our delight:
For all our good is in that primal good.
Concentrate and God's will and ours are one.

—*Dante, "Vision of Paradise."*

INTRODUCTION

In the investigation and application of astrology, particularly pertaining to mundane astrology, meteorology and the important problem of aiding the individual to find his place in the world, geographically as well as otherwise, who among professional astrologers and students has not felt the need of coordinating the heavens and the earth?

The solution of this astrologically important problem has engaged the author's attention for twenty years. After testing and discarding scores of equinoctial-geographic co-ordinates during this long period of research it is now believed a solution has been attained that will stand the severe tests of time— the critical check of history and the sound interpretive tests of the best astrologers.

There has long been a persistent notion among many astrologers that the vernal equinox co-ordinates Greenwich throughout all time. This, however, is a belief without astronomical foundation. It is easy to show, and astronomical texts do show*, that precession takes place not only on the ecliptic but also on the earth's equator, in the ratio of about $50''.25$ on ecliptic to $46''.10$† on equator. These values vary slightly and slowly as the obliquity of the ecliptic changes. Consequently, as the vernal equinox moves westward on the equator $46''$ per annum in right ascension or terrestrial longitude, it circles the earth in the equatorial plane in approximately 28,174 years $\left(\frac{360°}{46''}\right)$ and circles the celestial sphere in the ecliptic plane in about 25,800 years $\left(\frac{360°}{50''25}\right)$. Stated another way, the

---

* See Chapter I.
† Yearly rate for 1930, the epoch of Table I.

equinox circles from Greenwich to Greenwich on the equator
in the same period it circles the heavens along the ecliptic from
the meridian of the Great Pyramid to the pyramid again plus
to the Greenwich meridian. This significant fact is explained
in Chapter I.

Thus it was found early in the investigation that the co-ordination of celestial and terrestrial longitudes is not fixed, but
is a variable dependent on equatorial precession, 46″ per year.
In the course of about 28,174 years each degree and sign of the
zodiac must precessionally rise, culminate and set in turn for
any given city.

As the base adopted for the given table is: Greenwich
equals right ascension 29°10′ in 1930, it follows that the last
coincidence of Greenwich with the vernal equinox occurred
2,295 years* prior thereto, or in 365 B. C. Since then the
Greenwich meridian has advanced from 0° Aries to 1°19′ Taurus in 1930, and not until it has traversed the remaining arc
will it again coincide with the vernal equinox about 25,879
years in the future (28,174—2,295).

These values must not be confused with the correlative fact
that the cycle of equinoctial precession through the constellations in the ecliptic plane is only about 25,800 years. Failure
on the student's part to clearly comprehend this distinction between the terrestrial and celestial cycles can lead only to confusion in his application of the table of midheavens and ascendants, or lead him into wrong conclusions as to their rates of
yearly change in zodiac. Let him study carefully the explanation given in Chapter I.

In this drasticly condensed discussion of a vast subject no
complete arguments can be included to show the astronomical,
pyramidal and historical data by which the given co-ordination
has been derived. For such a purpose a large volume would be

---

* 29°10′ divided by 45″.8. The latter being the average equatorial precession
per year during the interval.

required. It is thought, however, that the diligent student will uncover much of the evidence for himself. The first aim of this text is to furnish a workable table which may be easily tested with world events, past or as they occur.

It is believed, however, that the suggestiveness of Leo, the lion, rising over Britain, France and Western Europe, with Taurus, the "John Bull" of European blundering diplomacy, on their Midheavens; the Virgo methodical characteristics of the German and Russian; the Libra inertia of India and Central Asia; the Scorpio secretiveness of the Chinese*; the Aries impetuosity of Western Americans; the Taurian phlegmatic temper of our Middle West; the Gemini ingenuity of the Eastern "Yankee," must all appeal to the thoughtful student as true of this general era in which he finds himself an observer. But since the Midheaven and Ascendant of any given location on earth completes one equatorial revolution in about 28,174 years, so all cities and nations rise and fall or pass successively through the changes of the signs.

Thus the jungle-buried and forgotten cities of the past come to light as men explore and marvel among the ruins of ancient splendors which are now no more, though may rise again. Not that each precessional cycle is identical. The "proper motions" of the so-called fixed stars slowly change each "celestial day," and thus beneath the seeming futility of the ages Evolution, the Snail, creeps noiselessly on.

---

* China's Ascendant was of course Libra 1000 to 3000 years ago—a period to which modern astrological copyists often turn for their authority. The same may be said of Aries as the Midheaven of England for over 2000 years prior to 1840 A. D., when the Greenwich meridian passed into Taurus.

CHAPTER I

PRECESSION

In view of the better understood fact that the rate of precession is about 50″.25 per year on the ecliptic at the equinoctial point, it seems advisable to illustrate how this becomes 46″.10 on the equator or in terrestrial longitude, and why the latter is the true basis of the corrective values for the cities' Midheavens and Ascendants.

Referring to Fig. 1, let AB define the unchanging* plane of the ecliptic. P is the north celestial pole around which N, the earth's north pole, recedes along M and completes a revolution during a precessional cycle; the south pole, S, likewise revolving along R in the same period. This causes equinoctial precession.

For illustration, let us assume N and S to be the plane of the earth's poles for the epoch 1930. Then EOF defines the equator and O is the vernal equinox on the zenith in terrestrial longitude NOS, which is given in Table I as 29°10′ West. Now let N′S′ define the earth's poles for, say, 2,000 A. D. The reader is to view N as rising perpendicular from the drawing to N′, and S as moved downward perpendicular to the drawing to S′. Owing to this movement of the poles the equator will have moved south at the vernal equinox as shown by ECF, and the point O, which is the equinox in 1930 in longitude 29°10′ West, will have moved to C, and the equinox will have shifted westward on the **ecliptic** from O to D and on

---

* There is a slight change in the ecliptic plane, due to **planetary precession**, but this is taken care of in the **general** precession cited presently.

4

the equator—that is, in right ascension or terrestrial longitude —from C to D.

The ratio of luni-solar precession on the ecliptic and on the equator is as OD to CD. Therefore precession on the ecliptic is given by the formula

$$(1) \quad 20''.05 \text{ cosecant } \omega = 50''.36,$$

wherein 20''.05 is the annual angular (OC) motion of the equator and ω is the obliquity of the ecliptic (angle CDO).

And the precession on the equator is given by the formula

$$(2) \quad 20''.05 \text{ cotangent } \omega = 46''.19.$$

When these values of luni-solar precession are reduced for the eastward shift of the equinox due to planetary precession the general precession for 1930 becomes 50''.25 on ecliptic and 46''.10 on the equator, this motion being to the west. The latter value changes 0''.028 per century; increasing after 1930, decreasing theretofore. The increase in the future will, of course, apply only so long as the obliquity of the ecliptic de-creases, as it will for over 300 years more. As we shall pres-ently see we need not concern ourselves with the change in the rate of ecliptic precession.

The reason CD, or equatorial precession, is the true correc-tive for the table of Midheavens and Ascendants is quite simple. Ephemeres for 1930 give the planets' daily longitudes as computed from O, the vernal equinox for 1930, in terres-trial longitude NOS or 29°10′ West, as per Table I. The ephe-meres for 2000 A. D. will give the planets' longitudes with ref-erence to D, the equinox of that period, and on earth this will co-ordinate with the terrestrial meridian N′DS′, or CD distance west of 29°10′ West. For such an interval

CO = (2000—1930) 46''.10 = 70 yrs. × 46''.10 = 54′

and,

N′DS′ = 29° 10′ + 54′ = 30° 04′ west longitude.

This means the Greenwich meridian in 2000 A. D. will be in right ascension 30°04', or in celestial longitude 2°15' Taurus instead of in 1° 19' Taurus as for 1930 in the table. This is an advance of 56' in ecliptic longitude in 70 years at this point of the zodiac.

Though precession on the ecliptic is 50".25 per year, or 58'.6 in 70 years, at the equinox, the student must not conclude this is the correct amount to advance the locality Midheavens at all points of the ecliptic in such an interval. Rather he must correct their right ascensions 46".10 per year and their longitudes by the values given in columns 5 and 7 of the table. He is to see that in this problem we are not concerned with the shift of the equinox among the constellations, except as it affects the positions of the fixed stars in the manner defined in the author's companion text thereon, but rather we are concerned with the shift of the equinox on earth, in order to maintain co-ordination between terrestrial meridians and the point of planetary reference in the ephemeres for different epochs, and thus co-ordinate the planetary longitudes and geographic longitudes. Thus, in column 5 of Table I, opposite the Greenwich meridian, we find '.80, and this multiplied by 70 years gives 56'. Adding this to the M. C. for 1930, 1°19' Taurus, we obtain 2°15' Taurus for 2000 A. D., as above computed from the elements of precession.

On first reading it may be difficult for the student to accept the statement in the introduction that the terrestrial cycle exceeds the celestial cycle by some 2,300 years, even though the ecliptic and equatorial rates of precession differ about four seconds a year, at the equinox. He is likely to wonder how two different equinoctial motions, setting out together from a fixed equinox and Greenwich in 365 B. C., can possibly bring the equinox to Greenwich again in about 28,174 years, when only about 25,800 years are required for a celestial cycle. The answer is the latter period is a sidereal cycle with reference to

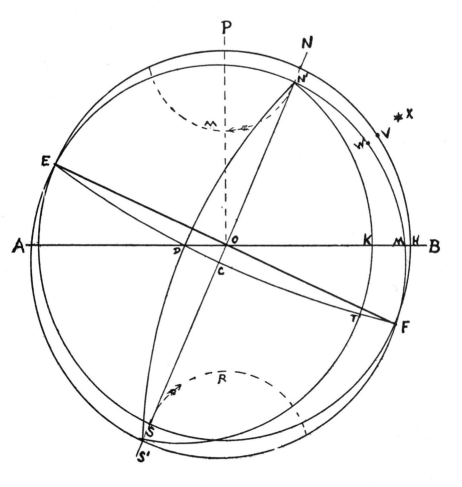

FIG. 1

the stars, not to the ecliptic precession of a longitude on earth.

Let us examine this more closely. As the equinox moves west on the equator 46″.10 per year, it is clear the right ascension of all cities must yearly increase by this amount. If a city's meridian coordinates the equinox, as is true of places in 29°10′ west longitude at this epoch, then its M. C. must advance 50″.25 per year in the ecliptic plane. But a place in geographic longitude 60°50′ East will be, at the same epoch, in R. A. 90° (29°10′ West plus 60°50′ East) or in 0° Cancer. At this point there are 65′.4 R. A. in an ecliptic degree, and such a city's annual ecliptic advance becomes

$$\frac{60′ \times 46″.10}{65′.4} \quad = \quad 42″.29,$$

and as its advance when at the equinox, some 7,000 years earlier, is 50″.25 per year, it is plain the average ecliptic precession of any city's M. C. during a quadrant or each quarter cycle becomes, approximately

$$\frac{42″.29 + 50″.25}{2} \quad = \quad 46″.27*,$$

the same as its R. A. advance on the equator. It thus requires 28,174 years for a geographic meridian to precessionally complete the cycle of the heavens.

In other words, a city whose M. C. is 0° Aries sets out at 50″.25 a year to complete a zodiacal revolution in about 25,800 years, but as the declination of the ecliptic increases to 0° Cancer this rate is gradually cut down to about 42″.29 at that point, and so its average advance along the ecliptic is only equal to the equatorial advance. In the next quadrant, from 0° Cancer to 0° Libra, the ecliptic rate of a geographic meridian gradually increases from 42″.29 to 50″.25 per year, and again the equatorial and ecliptic motions balance at the end of an

---

* This approximate equation of the average does not take into account the reduction for planetary precession. Hence it appears excessive.

other 7,000 years. And so the two complete cycles balance **on earth.** The **geographic** precession is constant on the equator and variable on the ecliptic because the relation of the R. A. plane to the geographic poles is fixed and both are referred to the movable equinox of the epoch. Thus a **city's M. C.** does not complete a cycle of the heavens in 25,800 years as does **a star** through the signs, but in about 28,174 years.

These periods are purely **relative,** not absolute, because the present precessional rates, 46″.10 and 50″.25, are in excess of the equinoctial rate throughout a **complete** cycle owing to the fact that the earth's poles do not process in a circle, and so the obliquity of the ecliptic, upon which they depend, is not a con-stant.

Drayson, contending the path of the poles to be an ellipse of six degrees eccentricity, computed the cycle to be 31,756 years and the maximum O. E. to be 35°36′. This would give the **average** yearly precession on equator as about 41″ through-out a cycle. While his argument is impressive and would bet-ter account for the glacial periods, it has not been accepted by astronomers, and it would in no way affect the **relative** facts above mentioned; nor would it affect the correctives of Table I for a few hundred years in the past or future, nor even very seriously affect them for a few thousand years. The present rate of precession and its reduction to any epoch within a few hundred or even a few thousand years, is based on a polar curve determined by astronomers from actual observation, and it is independent of any **theory** as to the actual path of the poles throughout a **complete** revolution.

Disregarding the Drayson theory and adhering, for sake of illustration, to the the more widely accepted polar curve, why does astronomy always refer to the 25,800† year cycle? Be-cause astronomy is not concerned with the problems of this text. It neither recognizes nor has need of any celestial and

---

† More exactly 25,827 to 25,868 years.

geographic co-ordination except that defined by **horary** time, latitude, declination, etc.

Let us examine this. Celestially speaking, R .A. precession at 0° Cancer is given by the formula

$$\eta \text{ cot. } \omega + \eta \text{ sine } a \text{ tan. } \delta^*$$

That is, by the sum of equatorial and polar precessions. This works out to about 55″. And since the R. A. precession at the equinox is 46″, the **average** advance in the R. A. of **a star** (disregarding "proper motion") becomes nearly the mean of these values, or 50″.25, the same as ecliptical precession at the equinox. Therefore the signs revolve among the **stars** in about 25,800 years.

Stated another way, we may say that the precession of a **geographic** point through the signs is affected only by the **equatorial** part of precession given by

$$\eta \text{ cot. } \omega,$$

which is 46″.10 for 1930, when reduced for planetary precession. The **polar** component of precession, which is expressed by

$$\eta \text{ sine } a \text{ tan. } \delta,$$

does not apply to this text because we are referring the geographic place to its ecliptic longitude from the **current** equinox each year, and because **the tilting of the earth's poles carries the city's meridian with it.** In problems of celestial precession, as of a star detached from the earth, the polar precession must be included when the celestial body is not on the equator. For a star having the R. A. and declination of 0° Cancer the annual polar precession is about 8″.7 in addition to the equatorial precession, 46″.10, or about 54″.8. At any other point in the quadrant and vertical to the ecliptic, the polar precession

---

* See Newcomb and Holden's **Astronomy**, page 212; or Campbell's **Practical Astronomy**, Chapter V.

is proportionally less, as may easily be seen from its formula,

$$\eta \text{ sine } a \text{ tan. } \delta.$$

The **average** works out to a cycle of about 25,800 years as earlier explained.

The difference in geographic (a city) and celestial (a star) precessional cycles is thus due to the fact that the **right ascensional plane on earth remains fixed with respect to the earth's poles, whereas the right ascensional plane in the heavens is constantly changing with respect to its previous plane because of the polar motion.**

This may be easily seen by referring again to Fig. 1. When the poles are at N and S and the equinox at O, any place in terrestrial meridian NFS, as V, is in right ascension FO (90°) and in celestial longitude OH (0° Cancer), and cotangent FO+cosine obliquity of ecliptic KOF; that is, an R. A. and longitude conversion table, defines the longitude of V in ecliptic. Let there be a star, X, on the celestial sphere vertical to V; then H is also the ecliptic longitude of the star. When the earth's poles have moved to N′ S′ and the equator has moved to C and the equinox to D, then K will define 0° Cancer, for that epoch, in right ascension DT (90°), and cot. DT + cosine TDK, or an R. A. and longitude conversion table, will define the point K, 0° Cancer, as readily as in the first instance it defined H. The right ascension of V will have advanced TF distance, equal to DC, or 46″.10 per year. But by the movements of the poles V will have moved to W, and its geographic meridian N′FS′ will then cut the ecliptic at M, so its ecliptic longitude will be DM and its ecliptic advance in the precessional interval will be KM, or MH (about 8″ per year) less than OD; that is as 42″.29 is to 50″.25 as earlier explained. But the star X, vertical to V, will not be carried to W by the polar motion NN′ and SS′, and so its right ascensional meridian NFS, with reference to a fixed equinox of sidereal reference, as O, will continue to cut the ecliptic at H, and its longitude at the second epoch will be DH or MH greater than the meridian of the place V when the tilt of the poles will have carried it to W. It is this difference that causes **the stars** to complete a **sidereal cycle** of precession in some 2,300 years less than the time required for a **geographic meridian** to complete a cycle through the **moving signs.**

The result is that each time the equinox and Greenwich coincide on the precessional dial, they do so some $33\frac{1}{2}°$ farther west among the stars or constellations, or a distance equal to the ecliptic longitude of the Great Pyramid from Greenwich. This may be shown by the following equation:

Longitude of Pyramid	31°10′	cot.	0.218369
Obliquity Ecliptic	23°27′	cosine	9.962562
Ecliptic equivalent	33°24′	cot.	0.180931

and,

$$\frac{360+33°24'}{50''.25} \quad = \quad 28,184 \text{ years,}$$

and,

$$\frac{360°}{46''} \quad = \quad 28,174 \text{ years.}$$

It is thus seen it was not by chance that the Greenwich meridian was chosen for astronomical reference thousands of years after the Great Pyramid had been built for that purpose in earlier times.

CHAPTER II

MIDHEAVENS AND ASCENDANTS

In Table I, given on pages 28 to 40, will be found the **precessional** Midheavens and Ascendants of over four hundred geographic points as determined from the Greenwich co-ordinate in zodiac and from their longitudes and latitudes, as computed and explained in Chapter III.

It is therefore to be understood these Midheavens and Ascendants in no way rest upon horary time or the diurnal rotation of the earth. **Rather they all stand or fall together because they are all computed from the Greenwich celestial equivalent and they all change with equatorial precession.**

Readers wholly unfamiliar with celestial and geodetic equivalents are here to understand that geographic longitude and celestial right ascension are measured in the same plane— that of the equator. The one is an earth measure of the equatorial circle and the other a "sky measure" in the same plane. The former is reckoned from Greenwich, the latter from the equinox or first point of Aries. But owing to precession the equinox shifts westward along the equator as explained in Chapter I, so that Greenwich and the equinox coincide but once in over 28,000 years. Planetary positions are given with reference to their distance eastward from the equinox. Therefore in order to co-ordinate their celestial longitudes or right ascensions with earth longitudes for the purpose of computing the longitudes of their affects on earth at any given time, it is necessary to know where the equinox is precessionally located on earth at the desired epoch, and from this as previously dis-

13

cussed we may then easily co-ordinate any geographic longitude with its true ecliptic degrees for any epoch.

In compiling Table I the epoch 1930 has been adopted,
with its proper corrective values, in order that the table will
serve with equal facility calculations on either the past or future with the minimum amount of labor and the least errors
arising from extending the corrective values over a century or
two either way, and also that the table may be the most accu-
rate for those whose limited training admits only of their observation of transits over the city angles in recent years and in
the immediate future. Very little effort is necessary, however,
to master all the astronomical facts and mathematical procedure necessary to revise this table for any distant epoch and to
direct the cities as will be later explained.

The explanation of the table follows.

Column 1 lists the national, state and provincial capitals
and other large cities, together with some smaller towns and
island points for the purpose of preserving fairly uniform con-
tinuity of co-ordination of all terrestrial longitudes in zodiac.
The Midheavens and Ascendants for places not listed are easily
computed as explained in Chapter III.

The cities are listed in the order of their right ascensions
and zenith longitudes in zodiac, rather than by country, in order to facilitate the observation of transits, eclipses, etc., on
their Midheavens. It would be desirable to repeat the listing
in the progressive order of their Ascendants in zodiac, but this
would greatly increase the cost. It is therefore recommended
that the student copy the Midheavens and Ascendants into
a book of chart blanks, adding the cadent and succeedent cusps
as approximately obtainable from Raphael's or Dalton's **Table
of Houses,** or working them out from Chaney's table of oblique
ascensions*.

---

* Chaney's **Primer of Astrology.**

Column 2 gives the **geocentric** latitudes of the cities as found from their geographic latitudes by Table II, which follows Table I.

Column 3 gives the cities' right ascensions in zodiac. These values **increase** 46".10† per year for epochs **after** 1930 and **decrease** at the same rate for periods **prior** to 1930.

Column 4 gives the Midheavens in zodiac.

Column 5 gives the rates of change in Midheaven longitudes per annum in terms of minute of degree expressed in decimal.

Column 6 gives the Ascendants in longitude as computed for geocentric latitudes. See further remarks on Ascendants presently. The Ascendants corresponding to the geographic latitudes; that is, to the spheroid, may be had by applying algebraically the values in column 8 to the values given in column 6.

Column 7 gives the Ascendants' rates of change per annum in terms of minute of degree expressed in decimal.

For the better understanding of those who may wish to extend the list of cities it may be said the corrective values in columns 5 and 7 are based on the expression

$$\frac{46".10}{R}$$

where 46".10 is the annual precession in right ascension and R is the ratio of right ascension and oblique ascension in one ecliptic degree at the points of Midheavens and Ascendants in zodiac, and in the latter instance in the latitude of the place. The value R in each case may be found by inspection of tables of right ascensions and oblique ascensions. Thus in an up-to-date R. A. table it may be seen that at 1° Taurus there are 57'.6 of R. A. in one zodiacal degree. This divided into 46".10 gives '.80 as the rate of M. C. change for London. In

---

† This value changes about 0".028 per century, decreasing before **1930 and** increasing thereafter as the obliquity of ecliptic decreases. **For very long** period use the **average** precession as so computed.

Chaney's oblique ascension table, pages 104-106 of his **Primer,**
we find in 17° Leo and for the latitude of London it requires
about 85'.5 O. A. for one degree of longitude, and this divided into 46".10 gives '.54 as the yearly rate of change of
London's Ascendant in zodiac, as shown in Table I.   The
values in columns 5 and 7 are **additive** after 1930 and **subtractive** for earlier epochs.

As example: Assume London's Midheaven and Ascendant are desired for either 1920 or 1940, the corrections become

ASC.   = '.54×10, or+5'.4 for 1940 and —5'.4 for 1920
M. C.   = '.80×10, or+8' for 1940 and —8' for 1920

The values in columns 5 and 7 are the current (1930)
rates of change.   Where greater precision is required for
periods very remote from this epoch, the change in ecliptic
positions of the Midheavens and Ascendants will so modify the
rate of their ecliptic precession that it is best to resort to the
more exact rule of adding or subtracting 46".10* per year to
or from the RAMC and from this calculate the M. C. and
Ascendant in the usual way from R. A. and O. A. tables.
The corrective values in columns 5 and 7 for 1930 will serve
all practical purposes for a few centuries, as in that time the
cusps are not sufficiently shifted in the zodiac nor the precessional rate, 46".10 sufficiently changed to materially affect
the result.

In most cases the computations of Midheavens and Ascendants were made from longitudes and latitudes listed in
geological and geodetic survey references.   A few places in
Africa, Asia, Alaska, and a few of the island points, were
scaled from maps owing to lack of more definite survey data.
It will be understood that large cities such as London, Paris,
New York, Chicago, etc., subtend within their limits some
10' to 15' of arc, as very roughly a mile on earth is a minute

---

* See footnote Page 15.

of arc. The points of reference used in computing the large cities are not necessarily central in all cases and a small allowance of 1' to 5' should be kept in mind in utilizing the table. This applies particularly to large cities. The Ascendants of large towns are also slightly affected for different north and south parts thereof, owing to the slight change in the oblique sphere.

The Ascendants were computed for the **geocentric** latitudes, as they best agree with such events as may be attributed to nature and are not due to direct human volition. These include the weather, storms, earthquakes, etc. However, when the Ascendant (or other **oblique** house) event is clearly very largely one of human volition, the Ascendant should be taken for the geographic **(gravity)** latitude if mathematical coincidence is expected to work out the more exact. Hence the values in the last column of Table I should be applied in such cases to column 6. Discussion of the reason for this, apart from observational tests, is beyond the scope of this brief work and is to be found in the laws of electrodynamics and electromagnetic waves as they relate to the researches of Biot and Kraft relative to the characteristics of spherical magnets and the distortion of the field force in spheroidal magnets—such as is the earth.

It may be added that Saturn usually responds to geocentric (spherical) angles, Uranus to geographic (spheroidal). This has been repeatedly verified. It is due to the fact that Saturn events are usually fatalistic, while those of Uranus most often involve the pragmatism of mankind. In other words, Saturn follows the electrical laws as they apply to solids or crystals— true geocentric patterns; whereas Uranus involves the laws of electromagnetic wave-form distortion due to, or in, such reflecting and absorbing mediums as gases, the surrounding atmosphere and organic forms*. Herein is a field for extensive

---

* See Morecroft's **Principles of Radio Communication** and other authorities on the characteristics of electromagnetic waves, and of dielectrics and conductors at high frequencies.

research.   The other planets have not been so well determined in this respect, as the investigation is rendered tedious because of the fact that the Sun's apparent diameter of 32′ has to be taken into account as will be discussed later.

It may be mentioned here that in order to greatly shorten the labor, the Ascendants were computed by Chaney's oblique ascension table.   Consequently, owing to the limited accuracy of all interpolative tables, some of the Ascendants may err 1′ to 3′ of arc from a true trigonometric determination.   Some of the very large cities have been computed by trigonometry as a check against this source of error, **but in view of the fact that most towns subtend an angle larger than this source of error,** and because of the waveband limits of influence represented by the Sun's apparent diameter, it was thought not worth while to resort to the tedious trigonometric formula in computing all the Ascendants; the more so as in the use of the world cusps   there are several other minor refinements which are quite beyond the scope of the present treatise, designed as it is for easy application for the beginner and for general purposes in mundane astrology.   In arriving at the base of the table† all the undiscussed minor correctives were applied, and it was found there remained now and then an apparent error of such regularity of amount as can as yet be explained only by the 16′ light channel subtended both ways from this basic mean by the Sun's semi-diameter as it centers on the equinox and with reference to the limits of eclipse contacts with the solar limb.   This point will be brought out later.

It is thought that once the student memorizes the sign on the zenith of each general longitudinal section of the earth, he will experience no delay in locating any city given in the table.

---

† Greenwich = 29°10′ R. A. in 1930.

Thus an index to the cities seems unnecessary.

While the Midheavens and Ascendants are tabulated in Table I for their **ecliptic** values, the student must clearly understand that every city or place has also a meridian and horizontal coupling with each planet's field plane according to its latitude at the time of an eclipse, its stationary, its aspects, its place at events and in nativities. These cannot be tabulated because they vary with the planets' motions. Such conjunctions must be computed in the manner of some of the examples in Chapters V and VI. This should be clear from a study of **Case 7,** Chapter VI and from inspection of Fig. 5, wherein it is shown that while Edison's BL Ascendant, taken in the ecliptic plane at Orange, N. J., is four degrees east of his Uranus, the coupling is exact in the field of his Mercury.

Therefore even in the observation of transits over the cities' Midheavens and Ascendants as given in Table I, allowance must be made for the deviation of planetary fields from the ecliptic, or else the transit must be computed in the latitude of the planet ruling the plane or field of the event. Thus any given transit over any of the electrical axes (house cusps) of a city expresses in at least nine distinct and significant events as the transit crosses the axis in the different planes of each planet, Sun and Moon, as these planes exist at the proper times of reference—eclipses, events, birth, etc.

Failure to recognize this fact has in the past rendered futile all investigators' attempts to reduce astrology to an exact mathematical science. Heeding this fact, and the use of the true Solar arc as hereinafter explained, removes all the mathematical disparities. Unfortunately it so increases the technicalities and the amount of necessary computations as to place directional astrology and the computation of the geographic focus of planetary couplings far outside the hope of application by the untrained mind.

These restrictions and limitations do not apply to the general analysis of nativities, nor to general or broad regional advisements on location or predictions of world events in an approximate belt or area. But to attempt to make astrology too easy is to debase it and destroy its usefulness. Few, indeed, realize the amount of calculation which goes into a true horoscope, the designing of an electric motor or the building of a modern bridge or skyscraper. The public notion of an engineer in any field is one who attains results without labor. This solely because the layman thinks in terms of results. He is not interested in cause or the manipulation of natural laws.

CHAPTER III

CALCULATING MIDHEAVENS AND ASCENDANTS

The examples given in Chapters V and VI will clarify the simple calculations necessary to solve the Midheaven and Ascendant of any place for any epoch, but it may not be superfluous to state the rule in detail and follow it with an example. It follows:

Set down 29°10′ R. A. as the Greenwich celestial co-ordinate for 1930. Correct this for equatorial precession at the rate of plus 46″.10 per year for the date if after 1930, subtracting at the same rate if the date is before 1930. To this corrected Greenwich base for the desired epoch **add** the geographic longitude of the place if it is **east** longitude; if **west, subtract.** The result is the RAMC of the place for the desired epoch. Find the corresponding longitude of the M. C. from this R. A. in a **table of right ascensions†**.

Then to find the Ascendant:

Rule 1—If the latitude of the place is **north.**

Add 90° to the found RAMC to obtain the O. A. (oblique ascension) of the horizon and convert this into ecliptic longitude under the pole of the place, using geocentric or geographic latitude as the case requires. The geocentric latitude may be found from Table II, which is self-explanatory. Geological survey references and maps give the geographic lati-

---

† Given in several standard astrological texts.

tudes of places, and the geocentric latitudes are always **less** by the amounts given in Table II.

Rule 2—If the latitude of the place is **south.**

Subtract 90° from the RAMC ,and having found the eclip-tic longitude of the resultant O. D., viewed as O. A., under the pole of the place, as in **Rule 1,** set down the degrees and minutes obtained, using, however, the **opposite** sign symbol— the same as in computing a horoscope for south latitude.

In applying these rules Chaney's table of oblique ascen-sions, given in his **Primer of Astrology,** may be used to con-vert O. A. into ecliptic longitude, or where greater precision is to be secured resort to the formula given on pages 204-205 of his **Primer,** or formula 1, page 259, of Pearce's **Text-Book of Astrology*.**

Example: What was the M. C. and geocentric Ascendant of Philadelphia for 1776, its longitude being 75°09' West and its geographic latitude 39°57' North? Solution:

```
   29°10'  R. A. Greenwich 1930 as per Table I.
  —1°59'  Precession 1930-1776 (154 yrs. × 46")
  ─────
   27°11'  R. A. Greenwich 1776
  360°00'  Add circle to subtract longitude
  ───────
  387°11'
  —75°09'  Longitude Philadelphia West
  ───────
  312°02'  R. A. Philadelphia in 1776   =  M. C. 9°36'♒
 +90°00'
  ───────
  402°02'
 —360°00'  Reject circle
  ───────
   42°02'  O. A. Ascendant,
```

which under pole 39°45' (39°57'—12', as per Table II) gives Ascendant 2°25'♊†.

───────────────────────────

* The beginner may of course find the approximate Ascendant for a town by inspection of a **Table of Houses** for the approximate latitude of the place, once he has computed its Midheaven as instructed on the preceding page.

† Equated from Chaney's O. A. table, **pages 80-82** of his **Primer.**

Or solving the Ascendant by trigonometry, we have:

O. A.	42°02′	cosine	9.870846
Lat.	39°45′	cotangent	0.080038
∠A	48ᶜ13′	cotangent	9.950884
O. E.	23°27′		
∠B	71°40′	a. c cosine	0.503318
	48°13′	cosine	9.823539
	42°02′	tangent	9.954946
	62°25′	tangent	0.281803
	—60°00′	two signs from Aries.	

2°25′♊ Ascendant of Philadelphia in 1776

In this case trigonometry and the interpolative method agree.

As Philadelphia is given in Table I, we may solve its Ascendant for 1776 much quicker as follows:

4°41′♊ Philadelphia Ascendant 1930
—2°17′ Precession for 154 years at ′.89 per year
2°24′♊ Ascendant in 1776.

This is as close an agreement as can be expected with a two decimal corrective for so long a period.

The beginner who is not familiar with the preceding equations can at least compute the Midheaven and then approximate the Ascendant from a **Table of Houses.**

As an example in computing the Midheaven of a geographic meridian for a more distant date, let us determine the longitude of the vernal equinox in 4004 B. C.

The interval from 1930 A. D. to 4004 B. C. is 5934 years, or 59.34 centuries. In a footnote to Chapter II, it was stated the **secular** change in the equatorial precession is 0″.028 per century. The **annual** rate of change in 1930 is 46″.10. Hence the average yearly rate of change for the interval becomes

$$46''.10 \; - \; \frac{59.34 \times 0''.028}{2} \; = \; 45''.28,$$

and the total precession of the equinox in terrestrial longitude
or R. A. during the interval becomes

$$\frac{5934 \text{ yrs.} \times 45''.28}{60 \times 60} = 74°38'$$

and,

74°38′ R. A. displacement of equinox
—29°10′ R. A. equinox West in 1930
45°28′ R. A. or geographic longitude **East**.

This longitude intersects the lower waters of the Tigris and
Euphrates rivers near the longitude of Kut-el-Amara, passes
through the Afrin ruins and about a degree east of Bagdad
and Babylon†.

From this it is seen the story of the Garden of Eden and
the legend of the beginning of the world in 4004 B. C., is
nothing more nor less than a corrupted form of the statement
of the astrologers of that time that the vernal equinox co-ordinated that region on earth. The word "world" is a derivative
from the much earlier word "whorl," to spin or turn, or make
revolution as from equinox to equinox. The "beginning of
the world in 4004 B. C.", means the beginning (first point of
Aries) of a whorl or precessional cycle, and the beginning of
the yearly cycle, co-ordinated that longitude at that time. The
Garden of Eden was the astrologers' point of equinoctial reference on earth from which at **that** period they computed
where the effects of a planetary or stellar configuration would
occur on earth.

The legend of the fall of the first man, Adam (Aries, the
celestial Ascendant) and first woman, Eve (Libra, the celestial
Descendant or evening angle), and their banishment from the
Garden, simply means the falling backwards or precessional
vanishment of the equinox from that region. The Angel
guarding the gate to the Garden against any return of the out-

---

† Also near Mt. Ararat upon which the Ark (arc, or equinox) rested.

casts, simply means the astrological and astronomical fact that the angles of the cardinal cross forever guard the entrance to Aries as it sweeps westward to annually meet the ascension of the Sun (Son) on the cross a short mile farther west each year. The equinox, now over the Atlantic, will reach America (New York) in about 3500 years.

In the same manner we may compute the time when the equinox was over India, and still earlier over China, and find in their legends the same story of the Creation or the beginning of a whorl or precessional cycle; the only significant difference in the tale being the attribution of the event to an earlier period, corresponding with the westward sweep of the equinox over those countries some 8000 (East India) and 10,000 (East China) years B. C. Those interested in this phase of the subject are advised to study Vail's **The Earth's Annular System.** While his approach was geological and biblical, his searching inquiry into the origin of early legends among widely separated racial tribes will be found very useful to those who wish to carry the calculation of the world horoscope back into the dawn of the human race.

As another example let us inquire when the vernal equinox was in the longitude of the Great Pyramid.

As the equinox is in 29°10′ west longitude in 1930 and the longitude of the Pyramid is 31°10′ East, their sum, 60°20′, is the precessional arc in right ascension or terrestrial longitude in the interval and the equation becomes

$$46''.10 \quad \frac{60°20'}{\dfrac{(47.81 \times 0''.028)}{2}} \quad = \quad 4781 \text{ yrs.}$$

and,

$$4781 - 1930 \text{ A. D.} = 2851 \text{ B. C.}$$

There is much dispute and speculation as to the time of the building of the Pyramid, but there is little or no disagreement

about its astronomical and astrological import. Various dates
have been assigned to the building, these ranging from about
1950 to 150,000 B. C.; but a majority opinion is that the building occurred some time between 2000 and 3000 B. C. Many
accept the date deduced by Piazzi Smith, namely 2170 B. C.,
but this finding has more astronomical than historical support,
and even its astronomical props depend on the assumption of
an unestablished fact—the **exact** path of the terrestrial poles
throughout an **entire** precessional cycle. There is in the whole
literature of astronomy not one conclusive proof as to what the
obliquity of the ecliptic was ten thousand years ago. Between
the accepted astronomical view and the able argument of Drayson there is a wide gulf, and until such time as observations
more completely establish the variables upon which precession throughout a **complete** cycle depends, we cannot hope
for too great accuracy in tracing the equinoctial co-ordinate on
earth back **beyond a few thousand years.**

The foregoing calculations, as also those of Table I, are
based on the constants and variables of Struve, and these
doubtless hold at least very nearly true for determinations
within the past 6000 years. That the Pyramid may have
been begun about 2851 B. C., when the equinox was about its
meridian, is in close agreement with the history of Egypt's
kings. A comprehensive analysis of pyramidal data is omitted
in the interests of condensation.

These citations are in no way offered as the principal reasons for the adopted base of the table of Midheavens and Ascendants for the present epoch; rather they are given as examples of how the base can be used in a study of the world's past.
Such calculations help to remind the reader that when the "ruling signs" were allotted to countries and towns by the early
astrologers the equinox and entire zodiac was one to two con-
stellation units farther east on earth than at present. For this
reason the modern astrologer errs seriously in his study of

world events when he adheres too closely to what was true "rulership" 2000 to 4000 years ago.

In many other phases of astrology the evils of the copyist equally prevail to mislead the student. If he is to get the most out of this volume he must break these bonds and recognize that all the great changes in the world, all human progress throughout a precessional cycle, spring from the fact that no mundane rulership is constant because of the slow sweep of the signs **westward** over the earth. As in other sciences, so in astrology, the truths of the past must be constantly modified to meet the changing conditions in the heavens and upon the earth.

Whenever a detailed study of a place is to be undertaken, it is, of course, essential to compute the mundo and zodiacal points of all fixed stars circling its geographic zenith and nadir in the latitudinal sense, as instructed and exampled in **The Stars, How and Where They Influence.** Also to ascertain by observation and past events which of these several stars **particularly** affect the place.

When it is desired to study the date of settlement or incorporation of a city, proceed as follows:

Place in a chart the position of the Sun, Moon and planets for the date of settlement or incorporation. Find the precessional Midheaven of the place for the epoch as instructed in the first of this chapter and as exampled by Philadelphia. Then progress this ingress M. C. on the solar arcs to the day of incorporation, after the manner of equations (4) and (5), Chapter IV. In other words, **treat the incorporation date of a city as you would the birthdate of an individual and compute its BL figure as in Chapter VI.** Progress the incorporation chart in the same manner as there instructed for nativities. Business incorporations may be considered in the same way. As also the beginning of any matter at a given place.

TABLE I—MIDHEAVENS AND ASCENDANTS—Epoch 1930

CITY	LAT. ° '	RAMC	MIDHEAVEN ° '		ASCENDANT ° '		'
29°10' West Longitude	0.00	0.00	0.00♈	.84	0.00	.00	0
Fayal, Azores	38.23N	0.26	0.28♈	.84	17.52♋	.63	+7
Brava, Cape Verde	14.42N	4.26	4.50♈	.84	9.59♋	.70	+2
Reykjank, Iceland	63.57N	7.15	7.54♈	.84	13.08♋	.48	+9
Dakar, Africa	14.35N	11.44	12.45♈	.84	16.30♋	.70	+2
Bathurst, Africa	13.23N	12.35	13.40♈	.84	16.48♋	.70	+2
Bolama, Africa	11.37N	13.43	14.54♈	.83	17.09♋	.70	+2
Freetown, Africa	8.19N	16.10	17.32♈	.83	18.04♋	.70	+1
Monrovia, Africa	6.17N	18.21	19.53♈	.83	19.18♋	.71	+1
Lisbon, Portugal	38.31N	19.59	21.37♈	.83	3.51♌	.61	+6
Oporto, Portugal	40.57N	20.32	22.13♈	.83	5.29♌	.60	+6
Limerick, Ireland	52.28N	20.33	22.14♈	.83	11.54♌	.53	+8
Cork, Ireland	51.39N	20.52	22.34♈	.83	11.39♌	.53	+8
Morocco,Africa	31.35N	21.27	23.11♈	.82	1.57♌	.65	+5
Londonderry, Ireland	54.48N	21.50	23.36♈	.82	14.18♌	.52	+7
Dublin, Ireland	53.12N	22.50	24.39♈	.82	13.57♌	.53	+8
Seville, Spain	37.12N	23.09	24.59♈	.82	5.47♌	.62	+5
Belfast, Ireland	53.59N	23.26	25.17♈	.82	14.50♌	.52	+7
St. Helena Island	15.49S	23.27	25.18♈	.82	15.22♋	.74	—3
Gibralter, Spain	35.56N	23.49	25.42♈	.82	5.45♌	.62	+5
Glasgow, Scotland	55.41N	24.52	26.48♈	.82	16.53♌	.51	+7

TABLE I—MIDHEAVENS AND ASCENDANTS—Epoch 1930

CITY	LAT. ° '	RAMC ° '	MIDHEAVEN ° '		ASCENDANT ° '		
Inverness, Scotland	57.17N	24.57	26.54♈	.82	17.20♌	.50	+ 8
Bingerville, Africa	5.06N	25.02	26.59♈	.81	25.03♋	.70	+ 1
Madrid, Spain	40.13N	25.29	27.27♈	.81	9.00♌	.60	+ 5
Edenburg, Scotland	55.46N	25.59	27.59♈	.81	17.41♌	.52	+ 7
Liverpool, England	53.12N	26.06	28.06♈	.81	16.11♌	.53	+ 7
Dundee, Scotland	56.46N	26.13	28.14♈	.81	18.28♌	.50	+ 7
Timbuctu, Africa	16.38N	26.26	28.27♈	.81	0.29♌	.70	+ 2
Bristol, England	51.16N	26.34	28.36♈	.81	15.23♌	.53	+ 7
Aberdeen, Scotland	56.57N	27.05	29.08♈	.81	19.08♌	.50	+ 7
Birmingham, England	52.16N	27.20	29.24♈	.81	16.29♌	.53	+ 7
Newcastle, England	54.48N	27.34	29.39♈	.81	18.08♌	.52	+ 7
Nantes, France	47.02N	27.37	29.42♈	.81	13.54♌	.57	+ 6
Lerwick, Shetlands	59.57N	28.01	0.07♉	.81	21.07♌	.48	+ 7
Nottingham, England	52.45N	28.02	0.08♉	.81	17.15♌	.53	+ 7
Portsmouth, England	50.36N	28.08	0.14♉	.81	16.07♌	.55	+ 7
Bordeaux, France	44.39N	28.35	0.42♉	.81	13.27♌	.58	+ 6
Valencia, Spain	39.16N	28.50	0.58♉	.81	11.14♌	.61	+ 5
Akkra, Africa	5.33N	28.51	0.59♉	.80	28.43♋	.73	+ 1
London, England	51.20N	29.03	1.12♉	.80	17.10♌	.54	+ 6
GREENWICH MERIDIAN		29.10	1.19♉	.80			
Havre, France	49.17N	29.17	1.26♉	.80	16.17♌	.56	+ 6

TABLE I—MIDHEAVENS AND ASCENDANTS—Epoch 1930

CITY	LAT.	RAMC	MIDHEAVEN		ASCENDANT		
	° ′	° ′	° ′	′	° ′	′	′
Toulouse, France	43.25N	30.36	2.47 ♉	.80	14.25 ♌	.58	+ 6
Lome, Africa	6.15N	30.37	2.50 ♉	.80	0.40 ♌	.72	+ 1
Barcelona, Spain	41.10N	31.21	3.35 ♉	.80	14.01 ♌	.60	+ 6
Paris, France	48.39N	31.30	3.45 ♉	.80	17.26 ♌	.56	+ 6
Porto Novo, Africa	6.38N	31.50	4.05 ♉	.80	1.58 ♌	.72	+ 1
Algiers, Africa	36.36N	32.13	4.29 ♉	.80	12.51 ♌	.62	+ 4
Ghent, Belgium	50.51N	32.53	5.10 ♉	.80	19.37 ♌	.55	+ 6
The Hague, Holland	51.53N	33.28	5.47 ♉	.79	20.32 ♌	.54	+ 6
Brussels, Belgium	50.39N	33.32	5.51 ♉	.79	19.58 ♌	.53	+ 6
Antwerp, Belgium	51.01N	33.35	5.54 ♉	.79	20.11 ♌	.53	+ 6
Lyons, France	45.34N	33.59	6.19 ♉	.79	17.56 ♌	.58	+ 5
Amsterdam, Holland	52.11N	34.03	6.23 ♉	.79	21.06 ♌	.52	+ 6
Utrecht, Belgium	51.53N	34.18	6.38 ♉	.79	21.07 ♌	.52	+ 6
Marseilles, France	43.07N	34.34	6.54 ♉	.79	17.19 ♌	.59	+ 5
Liege, Belgium	50.27N	34.44	7.05 ♉	.79	21.16 ♌	.53	+ 6
Geneva, Switzerland	46.00N	35.19	7.41 ♉	.79	19.07 ♌	.58	+ 5
Nancy, France	48.30N	35.21	7.43 ♉	.79	20.15 ♌	.56	+ 5
Zungeru, Africa	14.44N	35.57	8.20 ♉	.79	8.28 ♌	.71	+ 2
Cologne, Germany	50.45N	36.07	8.30 ♉	.79	21.51 ♌	.54	+ 6
Nice, France	43.30N	36.26	8.49 ♉	.79	18.54 ♌	.59	+ 5
Monte Carlo, Monaco	43.37N	36.36	9.00 ♉	.79	19.04 ♌	.59	+ 5

CITY	LAT. ° '	RAMC ° '	MIDHEAVEN ° '	'	ASCENDANT ° '	'	' +
Berne, Switzerland	46.45N	36.36	9.00♉	.79	20.24♌	.57	+ 5
Strassburg, France	48.24N	36.52	9.16♉	.79	21.19♌	.56	+ 5
Lucerne, Switzerland	46.51N	37.28	9.53♉	.79	21.04♌	.57	+ 5
Esbjerg, Denmark	55.16N	37.36	10.01♉	.79	25.03♌	.51	+ 6
Zurich, Switzerland	47.11N	37.42	10.07♉	.79	21.23♌	.57	+ 5
Frankfort, Germany	49.55N	37.51	10.16♉	.79	22.40♌	.54	+ 5
Genoa, Italy	44.13N	38.04	10.29♉	.78	20.26♌	.58	+ 5
Buea, Africa	4.44N	38.32	10.58♉	.78	7.41♌	.73	+ 1
Liberville, Africa	0.27N	38.43	11.09♉	.78	6.29♌	.75	+ 0
Hamburg, Germany	53.21N	39.10	11.36♉	.78	25.10♌	.52	+ 6
Kiel, Germany	54.09N	39.19	11.45♉	.78	25.39♌	.52	+ 6
Tunis, Africa	36.36N	39.20	11.46♉	.78	18.38♌	.62	+ 4
Odense, Denmark	55.12N	39.33	12.00♉	.78	26.19♌	.51	+ 6
Kristiana, Norway	59.43N	39.54	12.21♉	.78	29.08♌	.48	+ 6
Nuremberg, Germany	49.16N	40.14	12.41♉	.78	24.05♌	.56	+ 5
Florence, Italy	43.34N	40.25	12.52♉	.78	21.58♌	.59	+ 5
Munich, Germany	47.57N	40.47	13.14♉	.78	23.59♌	.56	+ 5
Venice, Italy	45.14N	41.31	13.59♉	.78	23.25♌	.58	+ 5
Rome, Italy	41.42N	41.39	14.07♉	.78	22.13♌	.60	+ 4
Copenhagen, Denmark	55.29N	41.45	14.13♉	.78	27.55♌	.51	+ 5
Boma, Africa	5.42 S	42.20	14.48♉	.78	8.00♌	.77	− 0

TABLE I—MIDHEAVENS AND ASCENDANTS—Epoch 1930

CITY	LAT.	RAMC	MIDHEAVEN		ASCENDANT		
	° '	° '	° '	'	° '	'	
Tripoli, Africa	32.42N	42.21	14.49 ♉	.78	19.45 ♌	.64	+ 3
Loanda, Africa	8.49 S	42.28	14.56 ♉	.78	7.04 ♌	.78	— 1
Palermo, Italy	37.55N	42.31	14.59 ♉	.77	21.35 ♌	.61	+ 3
Berlin, Germany	52.19N	42.34	15.02 ♉	.77	27.03 ♌	.52	+ 5
Windhoek, Africa	21.10 S	42.48	15.16 ♉	.77	2.35 ♌	.83	— 4
Dresden, Germany	50.51N	42.55	15.23 ♉	.77	26.40 ♌	.55	+ 5
Trieste, Italy	45.27N	42.56	15.24 ♉	.77	24.34 ♌	.58	+ 4
Naples, Italy	40.40N	43.25	15.53 ♉	.77	23.14 ♌	.61	+ 3
Prague, Czecho	49.54N	43.35	16.03 ♉	.77	26.46 ♌	.56	+ 5
Messina, Italy	38.00N	44.44	17.12 ♉	.77	22.48 ♌	.61	+ 3
Vienna, Austria	48.02N	45.30	17.58 ♉	.77	27.25 ♌	.56	+ 4
Bresleau, Germany	50.55N	46.12	18.40 ♉	.77	29.00 ♌	.54	+ 4
Stockholm, Sweden	59.09N	47.14	19.39 ♉	.76	3.03 ♍	.48	+ 5
Cape Town, Africa	33.48 S	47.50	20.17 ♉	.76	1.38 ♌	.89	— 7
Danzig, Germany	54.10N	47.50	20.17 ♉	.76	1.24 ♍	.51	+ 5
Cetinge, Montenegro	42.08N	48.06	20.32 ♉	.76	27.22 ♌	.60	+ 4
Budapest, Hungary	47.18N	48.12	20.38 ♉	.76	29.08 ♌	.56	+ 4
Belgrade, Serbia	44.36N	49.39	22.04 ♉	.76	29.19 ♌	.58	+ 4
Prisrend, Jugoslavia	42.00N	50.03	22.28 ♉	.76	28.49 ♌	.59	+ 3
Warsaw, Poland	52.02N	50.17	22.41 ♉	.76	2.15 ♍	.53	+ 4
Kalamata, Greece	36.49N	51.16	23.39 ♉	.76	28.19 ♌	.62	+ 3

TABLE I—MIDHEAVENS AND ASCENDANTS—Epoch 1930

CITY	LAT. ° '	RAMC ° '	MIDHEAVEN ° '		ASCENDANT ° '		'
Saloniki, Greece	40.25N	52.07	24.29 ♉	.76	29.59 ♌	.61	+3
Sofia, Bulgaria	42.27N	52.26	24.48 ♉	.76	0.48 ♍	.60	+3
Athens, Greece	37.47N	52.54	25.15 ♉	.75	29.50 ♌	.62	+3
Lemberg, Poland	49.39N	53.11	25.31 ♉	.75	3.31 ♍	.56	+4
Riga, Russia	56.45N	53.12	25.32 ♉	.75	5.56 ♍	.51	+4
Kimberley, Africa	28.32 S	53.56	26.15 ♉	.75	11.42 ♌	.91	−5
Port Elizabeth, Africa	33.47 S	54.48	27.05 ♉	.75	9.56 ♌	.92	−6
Lukanda, Africa	2.30 S	54.51	27.08 ♉	.75	21.49 ♌	.80	−0
Bukharest, Rumania	44.14N	55.16	27.33 ♉	.75	3.28 ♍	.59	+3
Bloemfontein, Africa	28.56 S	55.22	27.38 ♉	.75	13.14 ♌	.93	−6
Gallipoli, Turkey	40.12N	55.49	28.05 ♉	.75	2.50 ♍	.61	+3
Kalomo, Africa	17.12 S	55.50	28.06 ♉	.75	18.31 ♌	.87	−2
Smyrna, Turkey	38.15N	56.17	28.32 ♉	.74	2.43 ♍	.61	+3
Johannesburg, Africa	26.04 S	57.14	29.26 ♉	.74	16.48 ♌	.93	−6
Pretoria, Africa	25.38 S	57.21	29.33 ♉	.74	17.07 ♌	.93	−6
Constantinople, Turkey	40.48N	58.11	0.21 ♊	.74	4.54 ♍	.61	+3
Alexandria, Egypt	31.00N	59.03	1.11 ♊	.74	3.22 ♍	.66	+3
Leningrad, Russia	59.45N	59.29	1.36 ♊	.74	10.59 ♍	.49	+3
Peitermaritzburg, Africa	29.26 S	59.32	1.39 ♊	.74	18.04 ♌	.95	−5
Kiev, Russia	50.15N	59.40	1.46 ♊	.74	8.19 ♍	.54	+3
Odessa,Russia	46.17N	59.56	2.02 ♊	.74	7.31 ♍	.58	+3

TABLE I—MIDHEAVENS AND ASCENDANTS—Epoch 1930

CITY	LAT. ° '	RAMC ° '	MIDHEAVEN ° ' '	ASCENDANT ° ' ' '
Salisbury, Rhodesia	17.54 S	60.06	2.11 ♊ .74	23.11 ♌ .89 — 2
Novgorod, Russia	58.20N	60.26	2.30 ♊ .74	11.08 ♍ .49 + 3
Cairo, Egypt	29.50N	60.26	2.30 ♊ .74	4.20 ♍ .66 + 2
Ft. Jameson, Africa	13.19 S	61.37	3.38 ♊ .74	26.17 ♌ .87 — 1
Khartum, Africa	15.23 S	61.56	3.56 ♊ .74	26.03 ♌ .88 — 2
Jerusalem, Asia Minor	31.35N	64.23	6.15 ♊ .73	8.02 ♍ .66 + 2
Damascus, Asia Minor	33.20N	65.24	7.13 ♊ .73	9.11 ♍ .65 + 2
Moscow, Russia	55.33N	66.45	8.29 ♊ .73	14.28 ♍ .52 + 3
Adis Abeba, Africa	8.54 S	68.05	9.45 ♊ .73	4.40 ♍ .87 — 1
Zanzibar, Africa	6.09 S	68.22	10.00 ♊ .73	5.30 ♍ .86 — 0
Asmara, Africa	15.25N	68.27	10.05 ♊ .72	9.05 ♍ .75 + 1
Mombasa, Africa	4.03 S	68.50	10.27 ♊ .72	6.25 ♍ .84 — 0
Mecca, Arabia	21.16N	69.03	10.39 ♊ .72	10.33 ♍ .71 + 1
Mozambique, Africa	14.58 S	69.58	11.30 ♊ .72	5.36 ♍ .91 — 2
Tambof, Russia	52.32N	70.38	12.08 ♊ .72	16.32 ♍ .53 + 2
Totma, Russia	59.46N	71.56	13.20 ♊ .72	18.44 ♍ .48 + 3
Van, Turkey	38.18N	72.20	13.43 ♊ .72	15.41 ♍ .62 + 1
Bagdad, Mesopotamia	33.10N	73.32	14.50 ♊ .72	16.02 ♍ .65 + 1
Triflis, Caucasia	44.17N	73.39	14.56 ♊ .72	17.29 ♍ .59 + 1
Berbera, Africa	10.21N	74.08	15.23 ♊ .72	14.01 ♍ .77 + 0
Muscat Arabia	12.38N	74.09	15.24 ♊ .72	14.18 ♍ .76 + 0

TABLE I—MIDHEAVENS AND ASCENDANTS Epoch 1930

CITY	LAT.	RAMC	MIDHEAVEN		ASCENDANT		■
	° ′	° ′	° ′	′	° ′	′	′
Saratov, Russia	51.20N	75.14	16.24♊	.71	19.34♍	.55	+2
Tabriz, Persia	37.51N	75.29	16.38♊	.71	18.11♍	.63	+1
Tananarivo, Madagascar	18.48S	76.46	17.50♊	.71	13.11♍	.97	—1
Astrakhan, Russia	46.09N	77.12	18.14♊	.71	20.24♍	.58	+1
Teheran, Persia	35.30N	80.35	21.21♊	.71	22.10♍	.63	+1
Ispahan, Persia	32.28N	80.54	21.38♊	.71	22.14♍	.66	+1
Kerman, Persia	29.57N	86.20	26.38♊	.71	26.48♍	.68	+0
Orsk, Russia	51.01N	87.43	27.54♊	.71	28.23♍	.55	+0
Troitzk, Russia	53.53N	90.45	0.41♋	.71	0.31♎	.52	—0
Kelat, Baluchistan	28.53N	95.46	5.18♋	.71	5.04♎	.68	—0
Tobolsk, Russia	58.02N	97.27	6.50♋	.71	4.53♎	.56	—1
Tashend, Turkey	41.10N	98.19	7.38♋	.71	6.35♎	.61	—1
Kabul, Afghanistan	34.20N	98.20	7.39♋	.71	7.01♎	.64	—0
Bombay, India	18.47N	101.59	11.01♋	.71	11.23♎	.72	—0
Delhi, India	28.30N	106.23	15.06♋	.72	14.36♎	.68	—1
Colombo, Ceylon	6.53N	109.00	17.32♋	.72	19.35♎	.80	—0
Madras, India	12.59N	109.25	17.56♋	.72	19.10♎	.76	—0
Benares, India	25.09N	112.06	20.26♋	.72	19.59♎	.69	—1
Tomsk, Russia	56.19N	114.08	22.21♋	.73	15.55♎	.51	—3
Calcutta, India	22.15N	117.30	25.32♋	.73	25.19♎	.70	—1
Lassa, Thibet	29.28N	120.12	28.06♋	.74	26.18♎	.68	—2

TABLE I—MIDHEAVENS AND ASCENDANTS—Epoch 1930

CITY	LAT. ° '	RAMC °	MIDHEAVEN ° '		ASCENDANT ° '		'
Mandalay, Burma	21.54N	125.22	3.04♌	.75	2.30♏	.70	— 2
Rangoon, Burma	16.44N	125.23	3.05♌	.75	3.44♏	.72	— 1
Padang, Sumatra	0.58 S	129.31	7.07♌	.76	12.15♏	.78	+ 0
Bangkok, Siam	13.39N	129.41	7.17♌	.76	8.30♏	.72	— 1
Singapore, St. Set.	1.17N	133.01	10.34♌	.76	15.08♏	.76	— 0
Irkutsk, Russia	52.06N	133.26	10.59♌	.76	0.17♏	.53	— 5
Saigon, Indo China	10.43N	135.52	13.24♌	.77	15.10♏	.73	— 1
Batavia, Java	6.06 S	135.58	13.30♌	.77	20.23♏	.78	+ 0
Hue, Indo China	16.25N	136.49	14.21♌	.77	14.24♏	.71	— 2
Kuching, Borneo	1.21N	139.33	17.06♌	.78	21.33♏	.76	— 0
Canton, China	22.58N	142.26	18.00♌	.78	17.27♏	.68	— 3
Hong Kong, China	22.09N	143.19	20.55♌	.78	18.29♏	.68	— 3
Perth, Australia	31.35 S	145.03	22.42♌	.79	11.06♐	.80	+ 6
Pekin, China	39.42N	145.39	23.19♌	.79	14.15♏	.61	— 4
Tientsin, China	38.53N	147.29	25.12♌	.80	16.00♏	.61	— 4
Manila, Philippines	14.30N	150.08	27.57♌	.80	27.10♏	.71	— 2
Port Arthur, Japan	38.35N	150.14	28.04♌	.80	18.19♏	.61	— 5
Shanghai, China	31.04N	150.39	28.30♌	.80	21.41♏	64	— 4
Seoul, Korea	37.34N	155.45	3.51♍	.81	23.11♏	.62	— 5
Nagasaki, Japan	32.34N	159.01	7.19♍	.82	28.02♏	.65	— 4
Vladivostok, Russia	42.55N	161.03	9.29♍	.83	24.46♏	.59	— 6

TABLE I—MIDHEAVENS AND ASCENDANTS—Epoch 1930

CITY	LAT.	RAMC	MIDHEAVEN		ASCENDANT		
	° '	° '	° '		° '		'
Osaka, Japan	34.29N	164.37	13.18 ♍	.83	1.49 ♐	.64	— 5
Adelaide, Australia	34.35 S	167.41	16.37 ♍	.83	4.36 ♑	.70	+ 7
Yokohama, Japan	35.15N	168.49	17.50 ♍	.83	4.55 ♐	.63	— 6
Tokio, Japan	35.28N	168.54	17.56 ♍	.83	4.53 ♐	.63	— 6
New Guinea	5.00 S	170.10	19.18 ♍	.83	23.00 ♐	.70	+ 0
Guam Island	13.21N	173.49	23.16 ♍	.84	19.00 ♐	.70	— 2
Melbourne, Australia	37.39 S	174.09	23.38 ♍	.84	12.08 ♑	.66	+ 7
Sydney, Australia	35.40 S	180.22	0.24 ♎	.84	16.13 ♑	.66	+ 7
Brisbane, Australia	27.23 S	182.12	2.24 ♎	.84	13.34 ♑	.67	+ 5
Society Islands	16.21 S	188.20	9.04 ♎	.84	14.09 ♑	.69	+ 3
Noumea, Loyalty Ils.	22.08 S	195.37	16.57 ♎	.83	22.59 ♑	.68	+ 4
Wellington, N. Z.	41.07 S	203.56	25.49 ♎	.82	8.12 ♒	.61	+ 6
Aukland Island	36.39 S	204.00	25.53 ♎	.82	6.13 ♒	.62	+ 5
Wrangel Island	71.00N	211.10	3.24 ♏	.80	—		—
Chatham Island	43.37 S	212.28	4.45 ♏	.80	15.55 ♒	.59	+ 5
Samoa Island	13.40 S	216.53	9.17 ♏	.79	8.59 ♒	.70	+ 2
Bering Strait	65.00N	221.10	13.38 ♏	.78	—		—
Dutch Harbor, Alaska	53.42N	222.38	15.06 ♏	.78	6.08 ♑	.77	—17
Nome, Alaska	64.22N	224.02	16.30 ♏	.78	15.06 ♐	.50	—33
Palmyra Island	5.49N	227.00	19.27 ♏	.77	12.44 ♒	.80	— 0
St. Michael, Alaska	63.17N	227.10	19.37 ♏	.77	19.15 ♐	.56	—31

TABLE I—MIDHEAVENS AND ASCENDANTS—Epoch 1930

CITY	LAT. ° '	RAMC °	MIDHEAVEN ° '		ASCENDANT ° '		
Honolulu, Oahu	21.10N	231.20	23.43♏	.76	11.57≈	.88	—3
Christmas Island	1.57N	231.42	24.05♏	.76	18.43≈	.80	—0
Kalawao, Molokai	21.03N	232.11	24.33♏	.76	12.59≈	.88	—3
Wailuku, Maui	20.45N	232.39	25.00♏	.76	13.37≈	.88	—3
Hilo, Hawaii	19.37N	234.03	26.22♏	.75	15.38≈	.88	—3
Seward, Alaska	59.53N	239.55	2.01♐	.74	11.02♑	.92	—28
Fort Yukon, Alaska	66.22N	243.52	5.46♐	.74	19.00♐	.42	—52
Dawson, Yukon	64.00N	249.54	11.27♐	.73	7.36♑	1.0	—73
Sitka, Alaska	56.51N	253.50	15.06♐	.72	12.03≈	1.6	—26
Skagway, Alaska	59.16N	253.52	15.08♐	.72	7.11≈	1.7	—35
Juneau, Alaska	58.08N	254.47	15.59♐	.72	13.54≈	1.7	—30
Queen Charlotte Ils.	54.00N	257.10	18.12♐	.72	27.16≈	1.8	—18
Prince Rupert, B. C.	54.07N	258.54	19.48♐	.72	1.10♓	1.8	—16
Port Hardy, V. I.	50.31N	261.38	22.19♐	.71	10.58♓	1.6	—7
Cumberland, V. I.	49.28N	264.06	24.35♐	.71	17.02♓	1.6	—5
Nanaimo, V. I.	48.58N	265.10	25.34♐	.71	19.31♓	1.7	—5
Victoria, V. I.	48.13N	265.48	26.09♐	.71	21.08♓	1.7	—4
Vancouver, B. C.	49.05N	266.05	26.24♐	.71	21.28♓	1.7	—4
Salem, Ore.	44.44N	266.07	26.26♐	.71	22.35♓	1.5	—2
Olympia, Wash.	46.50N	266.16	26.34♐	.71	22.25♓	1.5	—2
Portland, Ore.	45.19N	266.28	26.48♐	.71	23.08♓	1.5	—2

TABLE I—MIDHEAVENS AND ASCENDANTS—Epoch 1930

CITY	LAT. ° '	RAMC ° '	MIDHEAVEN ° '		ASCENDANT ° '	'	'
Bellingham, Wash.	48.33N	266.41	26.58 ♐	.71	22.53 ♓	1.6	— 3
San Francisco, Cal.	37.36N	266.46	27.02 ♐	.71	24.43 ♓	1.2	— 1
Seattle, Wash.	47.24N	266.50	27.06 ♐	.71	23.27 ♓	1.5	— 2
Sacramento, Cal.	38.21N	267.41	27.53 ♐	.71	26.08 ♓	1.3	— 1
Reno, Nev.	39.19N	269.22	29.25 ♐	.71	28.55 ♓	1.3	— 0
Carson City, Nev.	39.00N	269.24	29.27 ♐	.71	28.55 ♓	1.3	— 0
Fresno, Cal.	36.33N	269.25	29.28 ♐	.71	29.03 ♓	1.2	— 0
Los Angeles, Cal.	33.54N	270.55	0.50 ♑	.71	1.24 ♈	1.2	+ 0
La Grande, Ore.	45.06N	271.04	0.59 ♑	.71	2.04 ♈	1.5	+ 0
Spokane, Wash.	47.28N	271.44	1.35 ♑	.71	3.36 ♈	1.6	+ 1
Tonopah, Nev.	37.54N	271.58	1.48 ♑	.71	3.15 ♈	1.3	+ 0
San Diego, Cal.	32.32N	272.00	1.50 ♑	.71	3.01 ♈	1.2	+ 0
Boise City, Ida.	43.25N	272.58	2.43 ♑	.71	5.31 ♈	1.4	+ 1
Wallace, Ida.	47.17N	273.15	2.59 ♑	.71	6.43 ♈	1.5	+ 2
Yuma, Ariz.	32.32N	274.33	4.11 ♑	.71	6.52 ♈	1.2	+ 1
Calgary, Alta.	50.50N	275.08	4.43 ♑	.71	11.53 ♈	1.7	+ 5
Edmonton, Alta.	53.22N	275.40	5.12 ♑	.71	14.40 ♈	1.9	+ 7
Butte, Mont.	45.51N	276.36	6.04 ♑	.71	12.55 ♈	1.5	+ 4
Pocatello, Ida.	42.40N	276.44	6.11 ♑	.71	12.10 ♈	1.3	+ 4
Phoenix, Ariz.	33.17N	277.06	6.31 ♑	.71	10.48 ♈	1.2	+ 1
Helena, Mont.	46.25N	277.08	6.33 ♑	.71	14.12 ♈	1.5	+ 4

TABLE I—MIDHEAVENS AND ASCENDANTS—Epoch 1930

CITY	LAT.	RAMC	MIDHEAVEN		ASCENDANT		
	° '	°	°	'	°	'	'
Ogden, Utah	41.01N	277.10	6.35 ♑	.71	12.29 ♈	1.3	+3
Salt Lake City, Utah	40.35N	277.16	6.40 ♑	.71	12.33 ♈	1.3	+3
Great Falls, Mont.	47.18N	277.55	7.16 ♑	.71	16.06 ♈	1.5	+3
Tucson, Ariz.	32.04N	278.11	7.31 ♑	.71	12.11 ♈	1.2	+2
Evanston, Wyo.	41.04N	278.14	7.34 ♑	.71	14.21 ♈	1.3	+3
Guaymas, Mexico	27.45N	278.17	7.37 ♑	.71	11.39 ♈	1.1	+1
Medicine Hat, Alta.	49.49N	278.33	7.51 ♑	.71	18.51 ♈	1.6	+7
Battleford, Sask.	52.29N	280.50	9.58 ♑	.71	26.11 ♈	1.7	+12
Albuquerque, N. M.	34.53N	282.31	11.31 ♑	.71	19.25 ♈	1.2	+3
Saskatoon, Sask.	52.03N	282.40	11.39 ♑	.71	29.42 ♈	1.7	+14
El Paso, Tex.	31.36N	282.41	11.40 ♑	.71	18.41 ♈	1.1	+2
Leadville, Colo.	39.04N	282.50	11.48 ♑	.71	21.16 ♈	1.2	+4
Casper, Wyo.	42.48N	282.52	11.50 ♑	.71	22.59 ♈	1.3	+6
Santa Fe, N. M.	35.30N	283.13	12.10 ♑	.71	20.36 ♈	1.2	+3
Denver, Colo.	39.33N	284.15	13.07 ♑	.71	23.44 ♈	1.2	+5
Cheyenne, Wyo.	40.56N	284.21	13.13 ♑	.71	24.32 ♈	1.2	+5
Pueblo, Colo.	38.06N	284.33	13.24 ♑	.71	23.36 ♈	1.2	+5
Regina, Sask.	50.14N	284.34	13.25 ♑	.71	1.36 ♉	1.5	+13
Roswell, N. M.	33.14N	284.38	13.28 ♑	.71	21.57 ♈	1.1	+3
San Pedro, Mexico	25.37N	286.11	14.54 ♑	.72	22.00 ♈	1.0	+2
Bismark, N. D.	46.36N	288.23	16.57 ♑	.72	5.05 ♉	1.3	+9

TABLE I—MIDHEAVENS AND ASCENDANTS—Epoch 1930

CITY	LAT. ° '	RAMC °	MIDHEAVEN °	'	ASCENDANT °	'	'
Pierre, S. D.	44.11N	288.50	17.22♑	.72	3.54♉	1.2	+ 8
Mexico City, Mex.	19.19N	290.03	18.31♑	.72	25.35♈	.95	+ 2
San Antonio, Tex.	29.17N	290.42	19.07♑	.72	29.08♈	1.0	+ 4
Hastings, Neb.	40.22N	290.46	19.11♑	.72	4.21♉	1.1	+ 7
Hutchinson, Kans.	37.52N	291.14	19.37♑	.72	3.37♉	1.1	+ 6
Tampico, Mex.	22.08N	291.21	19.44♑	.72	27.45♈	.96	+ 3
Austin, Tex.	30.05N	291.25	19.47♑	.72	0.22♉	1.0	+ 4
Oklahoma City, Okla.	35.17N	291.39	20.01♑	.72	2.54♉	1.1	+ 5
Wichita, Kans.	37.28N	291.50	20.11♑	.72	4.16♉	1.1	+ 6
Winnipeg, Man.	49.43N	292.02	20.22♑	.72	14.37♉	1.3	+14
Guthrie, Okla.	35.41N	292.05	20.25♑	.72	3.43♉	1.1	+ 5
Sioux Falls, S. D.	43.21N	292.22	20.41♑	.72	8.53♉	1.2	+ 9
Fargo, N. D.	46.41N	292.22	20.41♑	.72	11.46♉	1.2	+11
Dallas, Tex.	32.34N	292.23	20.42♑	.73	2.43♉	1.0	+ 5
Lincoln, Neb.	40.37N	292.28	20.47♑	.73	7.04♉	1.1	+ 7
Vera Cruz, Mex.	19.03N	292.52	21.09♑	.73	28.46♈	.93	+ 2
Tulsa, Okla	35.58N	293.10	21.26♑	.73	5.21♉	1.1	+ 5
Omaha, Neb.	41.04N	293.12	21.28♑	.73	8.27♉	1.1	+ 8
Topeka, Kans.	38.50N	293.27	21.42♑	.73	7.24♉	1.1	+ 7
Houston, Tex.	29.32N	293.50	22.04♑	.73	3.25♉	1.0	+ 4
Kansas City, Mo.	38.56N	294.35	22.46♑	.73	9.04♉	1.1	+ 7

TABLE I—MIDHEAVENS AND ASCENDANTS—Epoch 1930

CITY	LAT.	RAMC	MIDHEAVEN		ASCENDANT		
	° '	° '	° '	'	° '	'	'
Ft. Smith, Ark.	35.11N	294.48	22.58♑	.73	7.15♉	1.1	+ 6
Des Moines, Ia.	41.24N	295.34	23.42♑	.73	12.11♉	1.1	+ 8
Springfield, Mo.	36.55N	295.52	23.59♑	.73	9.40♉	1.1	+ 6
Minneapolis, Minn.	44.46N	295.55	24.02♑	.73	15.29♉	1.2	+10
St. Paul, Minn.	44.45N	296.05	24.11♑	.73	15.43♉	1.2	+10
Little Rock, Ark.	34.36N	296.52	24.56♑	.73	9.46♉	1.0	+ 6
Jefferson City, Mo.	38.24N	297.01	25.04♑	.73	12.11♉	1.0	+ 7
Duluth, Minn.	46.34N	297.06	25.09♑	.73	19.00♉	1.1	+12
Cedar Rapids, Ia.	41.46N	297.30	25.32♑	.73	15.16♉	1.1	+ 9
Galapagos Isl.	0.59S	297.42	25.43♑	.73	29.35♈	.81	— 0
La Crosse, Wis.	43.38N	297.56	25.56♑	.73	17.26♉	1.1	+10
Baton Rouge, La.	30.17N	298.02	26.02♑	.73	9.10♉	1.0	+ 5
Vicksburg, Miss.	32.09N	298.21	26.20♑	.73	10.28♉	1.0	+ 6
Dubuque, Ia.	42.17N	298.30	26.29♑	.73	17.05♉	1.1	+10
Guatemala, Guat.	14.37N	298.39	26.37♑	.73	4.23♉	.87	+ 2
St. Louis, Mo.	38.26N	298.58	26.55♑	.73	14.53♉	1.0	+ 8
Jackson, Miss.	32.10N	298.59	26.56♑	.73	11.18♉	.98	+ 5
Memphis, Tenn.	34.57N	299.06	27.03♑	.73	12.55♉	1.0	+ 6
New Orleans, La.	29.47N	299.07	27.04♑	.73	10.20♉	.96	+ 5
Springfield, Ill.	39.39N	299.31	27.27♑	.73	16.28♉	1.0	+ 8
Peoria, Ill.	40.30N	299.32	27.28♑	.73	17.07♉	1.0	+ 8

TABLE I—MIDHEAVENS AND ASCENDANTS—Epoch 1930

CITY	LAT. ° '	RAMC ° '	MIDHEAVEN ° '	'	ASCENDANT ° '	'	'
Madison, Wis.	42.52N	299.45	27.40♑	.73	19.19♉	1.1	+10
San Salvador, Sal.	13.35N	299.55	27.50♑	.73	5.32♉	.87	+ 1
Port Arthur, Ont.	48.15N	299.58	27.53♑	.73	25.25♉	1.1	+14
Belize, Honduras	17.23N	300.58	28.50♑	.74	7.52♉	.88	+ 2
Mobile, Ala.	30.30N	301.06	28.58♑	.74	13.10♉	.98	+ 5
Milwaukee, Wis.	42.52N	301.17	29.08♑	.74	21.25♉	1.0	+10
Chicago, Ill.	41.42N	301.33	29.24♑	.74	20.48♉	1.0	+ 9
Evansville, Ind.	37.47N	301.42	29.32♑	.74	18.06♉	.98	+ 7
Birmingham, Ala.	33.20N	302.22	0.10♒	.74	16.15♉	.96	+ 6
Nashville, Tenn.	35.58N	302.23	0.11♒	.74	17.50♉	.98	+ 6
Montgomery, Ala.	32.22N	302.52	0.39♒	.74	16.21♉	.98	+ 6
Managua, Nicaragua	12.00N	302.54	0.41♒	.74	8.24♉	.86	+ 2
Indianapolis, Ind.	39.35N	302.58	0.45♒	.74	21.03♉	1.0	+ 9
Louisville, Ky.	38.04N	303.24	1.10♒	.74	20.31♉	1.0	+ 9
Grand Rapids, Mich.	42.46N	303.30	1.16♒	.74	24.21♉	1.0	+10
Ft. Wayne, Ind.	40.54N	304.02	1.47♒	.74	23.26♉	1.0	+ 9
Frankfort, Ky.	38.03N	304.21	2.05♒	.74	22.25♉	1.0	+ 9
Lansing, Mich.	42.32N	304.37	2.21♒	.74	25.35♉	1.0	+10
Lexington, Ky.	37.53N	304.40	2.24♒	.74	21.59♉	.97	+ 8
Cincinnati, Ohio	38.56N	304.45	2.28♒	.74	22.53♉	1.0	+ 8
Atlanta, Ga.	33.25N	304.46	2.29♒	.74	19.16♉	.97	+ 6

TABLE I—MIDHEAVENS AND ASCENDANTS—Epoch 1930

CITY	LAT. ° '	RAMC ° '	MIDHEAVEN ° '		ASCENDANT ° '		'
Sault Ste Marie, Mich.	46.18N	304.49	2.32 ≈≈	.74	29.27 ♉	1.0	+13
Tallahassee,Fla.	30.16N	304.52	2.35 ≈≈	.74	17.41 ♉	.95	+ 5
San Jose, Costa Rica	9.50N	305.03	2.46 ≈≈	.75	10.05 ♉	.83	+ 1
Knoxville, Tenn.	35.46N	305.14	2.56 ≈≈	.75	21.16 ♉	.95	+ 7
Bay City, Mich.	43.25N	305.20	3.02 ≈≈	.75	27.36 ♉	.97	+10
Toledo, Ohio	41.28N	305.38	3.20 ≈≈	.75	25.57 ♉	.97	+ 9
Detroit, Mich.	42.09N	306.07	3.48 ≈≈	.75	27.08 ♉	.97	+10
Columbus, Ohio	39.47N	306.09	3.50 ≈≈	.75	25.14 ♉	.97	+ 8
Ashville, N. C.	35.24N	306.36	4.16 ≈≈	.75	22.43 ♉	.95	+ 7
Tampa, Fla.	27.46N	306.43	4.23 ≈≈	.75	18.40 ♉	.91	+ 5
Havana, Cuba	23.01N	306.48	4.28 ≈≈	.75	16.38 ♉	.89	+ 4
Augusta, Ga.	33.19N	307.12	4.51 ≈≈	.75	22.11 ♉	.94	+ 6
Cleveland, Ohio	41.18N	307.28	5.07 ≈≈	.75	28.05 ♉	.97	+11
Charleston, W. Va.	38.10N	307.32	5.11 ≈≈	.75	25.46 ♉	.96	+ 8
London, Ont.	42.47N	307.57	5.35 ≈≈	.75	0.00 ♊	.96	+10
Savannah, Ga.	31.54N	308.03	5.41 ≈≈	.75	22.24 ♉	.95	+ 6
Columbia, S. C.	33.49N	308.08	5.46 ≈≈	.75	23.37 ♉	.94	+ 6
Charlotte, N. C.	35.02N	308.19	5.56 ≈≈	.75	24.35 ♉	.94	+ 7
Wheeling, W. Va.	39.52N	308.26	6.03 ≈≈	.75	28.08 ♉	.93	+ 9
Miami, Fla.	25.39N	309.00	6.36 ≈≈	.75	20.20 ♉	.88	+ 4
Pittsburgh, Pa.	40.15N	309.10	6.46 ≈≈	.75	29.20 ♉	.95	+ 9

TABLE I—MIDHEAVENS AND ASCENDANTS—Epoch 1930

CITY	LAT. ° ′	RAMC ° ′	MIDHEAVEN ° ′	′	ASCENDANT ° ′	′	′
Colon, Panama	9.17N	309.17	6.53 ♒	.75	14.28 ♉	.81	+ 1
Charleston, S. C.	32.34N	309.20	6.56 ♒	.76	24.19 ♉	.90	+ 6
Panama, Panama	8.54N	309.38	7.14 ♒	.76	14.42 ♉	.81	+ 1
Toronto, Ont.	43.28N	309.46	7.22 ♒	.76	2.50 ♊	.93	+10
Lynchburg, Va.	37.14N	310.01	7.36 ♒	.76	28.05 ♉	.92	+ 8
Buffalo, N. Y.	42.41N	310.17	7.52 ♒	.76	2.47 ♊	.93	+10
Quito, Equador	0.14S	310.27	8.02 ♒	.76	12.56 ♉	.78	— 0
Raleigh, N. C.	35.37N	310.34	8.09 ♒	.76	27.39 ♉	.91	+ 7
Wilmington, N. C.	34.02N	311.13	8.47 ♒	.76	27.23 ♉	.91	+ 7
Rochester, N. Y.	42.57N	311.33	9.07 ♒	.76	4.31 ♊	.91	+10
Richmond, Va.	37.22N	311.42	9.16 ♒	.76	0.11 ♊	.91	+ 8
Nassau, Bahamas	24.57N	311.44	9.18 ♒	.76	23.08 ♉	.87	+ 4
Lima, Peru	12.00S	312.09	9.42 ♒	.76	11.15 ♉	.72	— 1
WASHINGTON, D. C.	38.42N	312.10	9.43 ♒	.76	1.43 ♊	.93	+ 8
Harrisburg, Pa.	40.04N	312.17	9.50 ♒	.76	2.56 ♊	.92	+ 9
Wilkes-Barre, Pa.	41.03N	312.17	9.50 ♒	.76	3.44 ♊	.92	+ 9
Kingston, Jamaica	17.51N	312.22	9.55 ♒	.76	20.48 ♉	.84	+ 3
Baltimore, Md.	39.04N	312.35	10.08 ♒	.76	2.30 ♊	.91	+ 9
Annapolis, Md.	38.47N	312.41	10.14 ♒	.76	2.24 ♊	.91	+ 9
Kingston, Ont.	44.01N	312.44	10.17 ♒	.76	6.56 ♊	.91	+12
Norfolk, Va.	36.41N	312.54	10.27 ♒	.76	1.07 ♊	.90	+ 9

TABLE I—MIDHEAVENS AND ASCENDANTS—Epoch 1930

CITY	LAT.	RAMC	MIDHEAVEN		ASCENDANT		
	° '	°	° '	'	° '	'	'
Syracuse, N. Y.	42.51N	313.01	10.34♒	.76	6.10♊	.91	+11
Santiago, Cuba	19.50N	313.18	10.51♒	.76	22.35♉	.84	+ 3
Ottawa, Ont.	45.14N	313.28	11.00♒	.76	8.58♊	.88	+12
Dover, Del.	38.58N	313.39	11.12♒	.77	3.40♊	.88	+10
Philadelphia, Pa.	39.45N	314.01	11.33♒	.77	4.41♊	.89	+10
Trenton, N. J.	40.01N	314.26	11.58♒	.77	5.21♊	.90	+10
Atlantic City, N. J	39.02N	314.49	12.21♒	.77	5.02♊	.89	+10
Bogota, Columbia	4.42N	314.58	12.30♒	.77	18.53♉	.77	+ 1
Newark, N. J.	40.32N	315.00	12.32♒	.77	6.27♊	.89	+10
NEW YORK, N. Y.	40.32N	315.09	12.41♒	.77	6.37♊	.89	+10
La Paz, Bolivia	16.25 S	315.25	12.57♒	.77	13.04♉	.71	— 2
Albany, N. Y.	42.28N	315.25	12.57♒	.77	8.33♊	.86	+10
Montreal, Que.	45.19N	315.37	13.09♒	.77	11.29♊	.86	+12
Burlington, Vt.	44.17N	315.58	13.30♒	.77	10.52♊	.88	+12
Bridgeport, Conn.	40.59N	315.59	13.31♒	.77	7.57♊	.88	+10
New Haven, Conn.	41.06N	316.15	13.47♒	.77	8.18♊	.87	+10
Hartford, Conn.	41.32N	316.30	14.02♒	.77	8.57♊	.86	+10
Springfield, Mass.	41.54N	316.35	14.07♒	.77	9.22♊	.86	+10
Montpelier, Vt.	44.03N	316.38	14.10♒	.77	11.23♊	.86	+11
Port au Prince, Hayti	18.27N	316.48	14.20♒	.77	25.53♉	.81	+ 4
Manchester, N. H.	42.48N	317.41	15.13♒	.77	11.23♊	.85	+10

TABLE I—MIDHEAVENS AND ASCENDANTS—Epoch 1930

CITY	LAT. °	RAMC ° '	MIDHEAVEN ° '	'	ASCENDANT ° '	'	'
Concord, N. H.	43.00N	317.41	15.13 ≈	.77	11.33 ♊	.85	+10
Providence, R. I.	41.38N	317.46	15.18 ≈	.77	10.21 ♊	.85	+10
Quebec, Que.	46.36N	317.57	15.29 ≈	.77	15.23 ♊	.85	+12
Fall River, Maass.	41.30N	318.00	15.32 ≈	.77	10.46 ♊	.85	+10
Boston, Mass.	42.10N	318.06	15.38 ≈	.77	11.17 ♊	.85	+10
Plymouth, N. H.	42.52N	318.27	15.59 ≈	.77	12.16 ♊	.83	+10
Santiago, Chile	33.16 S	318.29	16.01 ≈	.77	10.44 ♉	.65	— 3
Portland, Me.	43.27N	318.53	16.25 ≈	.77	13.15 ♊	.82	+10
Santo Domingo, Hayti	18.21N	319.17	16.50 ≈	.77	28.23 ♉	.81	+ 3
Augusta, Me.	44.09N	319.20	16.53 ≈	.77	14.24 ♊	.82	+11
Bangor, Me.	44.36N	320.23	17.56 ≈	.78	15.58 ♊	.82	+11
Fredericton, N. B.	45.43N	321.35	19.09 ≈	.78	18.19 ♊	.80	+12
Caracas, Venezuela	10.27N	322.16	19.51 ≈	.78	28.17 ♉	.77	+ 1
San Juan, Porto Rico	18.22N	323.02	20.38 ≈	.78	2.17 ♊	.78	+ 3
St. John, N. B.	45.05N	323.06	20.42 ≈	.78	19.17 ♊	.80	+12
Sucre, Bolivia	18.53 S	323.58	21.35 ≈	.78	20.07 ♉	.69	— 2
Dock Yards, Bermuda	32.09N	324.21	21.59 ≈	.79	10.41 ♊	.80	+ 7
Charlottetown, P. E. I.	46.02N	326.01	23.41 ≈	.79	23.07 ♊	.76	+12
Halifax, N. S.	46.28N	326.45	24.27 ≈	.80	24.16 ♊	.75	+12
Port of Spain, Tr.	10.34N	327.39	25.23 ≈	.80	3.45 ♊	.77	+ 1
Sydney, N. S.	45.58N	329.00	26.47 ≈	.80	25.57 ♊	.74	+12

TABLE I.—MIDHEAVENS AND ASCENDANTS—Epoch 1930

CITY	LAT.	RAMC	MIDHEAVEN ° '	MIDHEAVEN '	ASCENDANT ° '	ASCENDANT '	ASCENDANT
Bridgetown, Bar.	13.04N	329.35	27.23 ≈	.80	6.40 Π	.77	+ 1
Buenos Aires, Arg.	34.25 S	330.48	28.39 ≈	.80	20.30 ♉	.63	— 4
Georgetown, Br. Gu.	6.34N	331.08	29.00 ≈	.80	5.37 Π	.75	+ 1
Port Stanley, Falk.	51.29 S	331.19	29.11 ≈	.80	13.02 ♉	.54	— 6
Asuncion, Paraguay	25.06 S	331.29	29.22 ≈	.80	24.38 ♉	.67	— 3
Montevideo, Uruguay	34.44 S	332.58	0.55 ✶	.80	22.08 ♉	.63	— 4
Paramaribo, Dt. Gu.	5.38N	334.01	2.01 ✶	.81	8.03 Π	.74	+ 1
Cayenne, Fr. Gu.	4.54N	336.50	5.00 ✶	.82	10.27 Π	.74	+ 1
Para, Brazil	1.27 S	340.40	9.04 ✶	.82	11.37 Π	.72	— 0
St. Johns, Nfd.	47.22N	341.36	10.04 ✶	.83	8.34 ♋	.66	+11
Rio de Janeiro, Br.	22.46 S	346.00	14.48 ✶	.84	9.10 Π	.67	— 3
Bahia, Brazil	12.53 S	350.39	19.50 ✶	.84	16.20 Π	.70	— 2
Pernambuco, Br.	8.01 S	354.18	23.47 ✶	.84	21.35 Π	.71	— 1
Flores, Azores	39.20N	357.57	27.46 ✶	.84	16.21 ♋	.65	+ 7

TABLE II

GEOGRAPHIC—GEOCENTRIC CONVERSION TABLE

Lat. °	± ′ ″	Lat. °	Lat. °	± ′ ″	Lat. °
0	0 00	90	23	8 25	67
1	0 25	89	24	8 42	66
2	0 50	88	25	8 58	65
3	1 14	87	26	9 14	64
4	1 38	86	27	9 29	63
5	2 02	85	28	9 43	62
6	2 26	84	29	9 56	61
7	2 50	83	30	10 09	60
8	3 13	82	31	10 21	59
9	3 37	81	32	10 32	58
10	4 00	80	33	10 42	57
11	4 22	79	34	10 52	56
12	4 45	78	35	11 01	55
13	5 07	77	36	11 09	54
14	5 29	76	37	11 16	53
15	5 50	75	38	11 23	52
16	6 11	74	39	11 28	51
17	6 32	73	40	11 33	50
18	6 53	72	41	11 37	49
19	7 12	71	42	11 40	48
20	7 31	70	43	11 42	47
21	7 50	69	44	11 43	46
22	8 08	68	45	11 44	45

These values are constant for all epochs

REMARKS

The columns marked ± give the difference between geographic and geocentric values for the corresponding latitude. If the table is consulted with geographic latitude **subtract** the value in corresponding ± column to obtain geocentric latitude.

If the table is consulted with geocentric latitude **add** the corrective value to obtain geographic value.

It will be noted the diff. is maximum at 45°N or S, and above that latitude the diff. decreases at the same rate.

Thus for 10° and 80° the conversion value is 4′00″. For 30° and 60° it is 10′09″.

CHAPTER IV

USE OF LOCALITY ANGLES

It must not be assumed that all great events of a city or locality may be read simply by inspection of planetary transits over their Midheavens and Ascendants as given in Table I. **This would be far, indeed, from the truth.** The careful student will compute, or plot from **Tables of Houses,** all the twelve* cusps of places he wishes to study in detail. For not all things come under the rule of the Midheaven (government, business, etc.) nor Ascendant (life and disposition of the people, etc). For instance, if a detailed study of earthquakes, mining or real estate, or even underworld conditions, is to be undertaken, the Nadir must receive much attention. Or if the investigation pertains to speculative markets the 2nd, 5th, 8th and 11th cusps must not be neglected. The 7th cusp must be considered as to marriage customs, the divorce rate, etc. The 3rd house to postal affairs and road questions. And so on.

It is not within the scope of this condensed volume to instruct in the rulership of the various house angles. Of this much has been repeatedly given in the standard astrological texts, most of it sound insofar as it goes and much more remains to be learned and recorded. Compelled by lack of space to leave house rulership to the individual reader's previous training and discernment, it is imperative, however, to point out certain other facts concerning the use of the locality cusps.

---

* In strict truth there are **twenty-four** cusps or hour ("our") angles to be considered, but to cite the other twelve in this work might to many appear as an invention of the author's to conceal some short-coming of the base of Table 1. Their discussion belongs to **another text.**

In the first place, the Midheavens and Ascendants as given for 1930 in Table I, and to be corrected to any other epoch as has been explained in earlier chapters, are to be viewed as **the precessional meridians and horizons of the cities for the time of ingress (Sun 0° Aries),** the astrological beginning of the year. As previously stated, these cusps* revolve **precessionally** in the **equatorial** or terrestrial longitude plane in about 28,174 years. But they also revolve annually by **apparent** solar motion, really by the earth's orbital revolution. This last statement means the Midheavens and Ascendants may be, and must be, **directed on the Placidian arc to the dates of eclipses, planetary stationaries, great conjunctions and oppositions, new moons and events†.** Of these dates the eclipses should receive major attention, secondly the stationary times of the most massive planets, and thirdly the date of event. As the electrodynamic explanation of eclipses and planetary stationaries is given in the author's companion work **The Stars, How and Where they Influence,** it is unnecessary to repeat this in the present work, as these texts are so intimately interlocking in the problem of localizing planetary and stellar influences on earth as to be equally indispensable to those who wish to attain a fuller knowledge of mundane astrology and of the engineering of individual lives to their geographic points of greatest success in any given aim.

---

* For the better understanding of readers unfamiliar with astrological terminology, it may here be said the term "cusp" means the beginning of a "house" of an astrological figure, and a "house" is a two-hour space, or multiple thereof, measured from the meridian. Thus the "cusp of the Ascendant" is the point at which the horizon of a given latitude and longitude intersects the ecliptic or plane of the earth's orbit. Such astrological terms as "cusp," "house" and "aspect" are unfortunate, as they obscure to the average trained and untrained mind the one electrophysical fact which all these terms symbolize; namely, the electrical axes met with in all investigations of crystallography, atomic and molecular structures, oscillating and rectifying crystals, and, in short in every consideration of the rotation of the Cartesian co-ordinates of the three-dimensional form world in the "energy field" which constitutes the four-dimensional time-space or continuum.

† For computing the directional arc of eclipses, events or elective times see page 57 this chapter. For the true modification of the Placidian equation as applicable to both BL figures and nativities see Chapter VI, Case 2.

How the locality cusps or electric axes of a city for the time of an eclipse or event are actually computed by the foregoing principle will be made clear by the examples in the following chapters, remembering that as the earth, or the apparent Sun, moves about a degree a day the annular progression of the in-gress cusps, of Table I advance at the same rate. Therefore the progressed cusps at **events** cannot be computed nearer than some part of a degree unless the hour of event is known from which to equate the Sun's exact longitude. As we shall pres-ently see, we are not concerned with **horary** time except as it effects the length of the solar arc. This does not mean the use of purely **horary** figures of eclipses, etc., nor the hours of births, are to be ignored in the usual work covered by stand-ard astrological texts. It merely means this treatise deals with cosmic (precessional) and annular time, **and would hold true even if the earth did not daily revolve on its axis at all, but merely nodding on its poles drifted around the Sun with but one diurnal revolution,** as the Moon drifts around the earth. As the Sun's longitude can be computed exactly for the times of eclipses, planetary stationaries, etc., the cusps can be di-rected on the solar arc to precision for such phenomena, even though the **hour** of events induced by their electromagnetic couplings with planets during the year may not in all cases be known.

To clarify the direction of the locality cusps of the ingress as they have been determined on the precessional dial as in Table I, or as computed as exampled in Chapter III, let us refer to Fig. 2 for a better understanding how the solar arc ad-vances them around the ecliptic from month to month in their **annual** progression. In this heliocentric diagram A is the po-sition of the earth when the Sun appears in line with the ver-nal equinox in the direction of C. When the Sun appears to enter Cancer at D the earth is really at B. And so on around the figure.

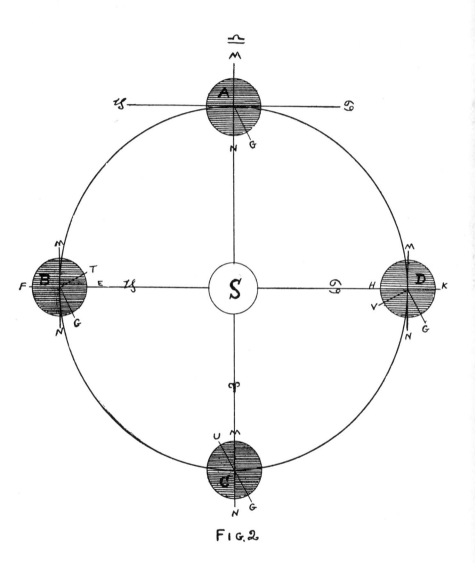

FIG. 2

Now since in this entire problem of locality horoscopes we are not concerned with horary time, except as it affects the Sun's longitude in determining the solar arc of progression as above explained, let the reader forget diurnal motion and think of the earth as drifting without axial rotation from A to B, C, D and back to A during the year. Then as A is the position of the earth at the time of the Sun's entrance into Aries, it should be clear that M, 0° Libra, becomes for that time according to Table I, the Midheaven of all places in long-itude 180°00'—29°10' West, or in 150°50' East; near the mer-idian of Sydney, Australia, for instance, as may be seen in Table I. Further, N represents the equinox, 0° Aries, in 29°10' West, and G represents the Greenwich meridian point-ing to 1°19' Taurus in R. A. 29°10' east of the equinox.

It will now be seen that when the earth arrives at B, C and D at three month intervals on the **annular** dial the three **precessional** meridians M, N, G, on the **sidereal** dial will point in the same direction in space as when the earth is at A, even though in horary figures they must point quite differ-ently when the earth each year arrives at these points in its orbit. Let us repeat that this treatise is concerned with pre-cessional and annual cycles and is not to be confused with hor-ary or diurnal time.

Now although at B, C and D the Greenwich meridian will, in the precessional sense, still point to 1°19' Taurus throughout the year, **something else has occurred which is the very foundation of solar arc directing, no less in nativities than in the present problem of the world horoscope.** It is this: When the earth is at A the line NM represents **the di-rection in which the Sun's radial electric field threads the earth,** the line GA represents **the direction of the earth's radial electric field at the Greenwich meridian,** and the angle GAN defines the interlinkage of the Sun's and earth's radial fields at that meridian; that is to say, **their degree of constant coupling or mutual induction† at Greenwich.**

When the earth arrives at B and the Sun appears on the summer solstice in the direction D, the Sun's radial electric field, pulsing at light frequencies, will meet the earth in the line EF, having changed its inductive coupling with the earth's field by 90° **for any given meridian on earth,** or swept the earth from N to E. Therefore the phase GAN at A is advanced to EBT at B, and to retain the constant inductive coupling for that time of the year we must advance the Greenwich meridian to T. At C the Sun's radial field will have swept through 180° of the earth and to retain the same inductive relations Greenwich must be advanced from G to U, and at D from G to V. In other words the more complete electrical expression of the phenomena, which is too technical for this simple presentation, is such that it is **as though** the earth moved around the Sun and presented the same meridian or side to the Sun at all times, as is the case of the Moon about the earth.

As the **magnetic** field of the Sun's light waves is perpendicular to their **electric** field, and both are perpendicular to the radial propagation of the light waves in the line of the earth's radius vector*, what really concerns us for the moment is the advance of the Sun's light waves' **magnetic** field around the earth as the earth advances in its orbit. This cannot be shown in Fig. 2, as the magnetic field is not in the plane of the drawing, but lies in the plane of the celestial poles and is defined in Fig. 7 in **The Stars, How and Where They Influence,** by the line DX. In Fig. 2 of the present work the magnetic field of the Sun's light waves would be per-

---

† See Morecroft's **Principles of Radio Communication** and other works on electromagnetism. Also **The Stars, How and Where They Influence,** Chapter XI.

* See Morecroft's **Principles of Radio Communication,** page 318. Also the author's companion work, **The Stars,** Figs. 5 and 6, Chapter XI.

pendicular to the plane of the drawing, the latter being the plane of the **electric** field or ecliptic, and corresponds to PC, Fig. 7, in the other text.

It will serve those of a little electrical training to think of this magnetic-field advance around the earth, as it moves in its orbit, as similar to advancing the pole pieces of a dynamo or motor. They will see at once that the points of commutation must be likewise advanced in the plane of armature rotation, that is to say, in our cosmic generator **the Sun's proportional advance in right ascension must be taken as one of the arcs of direction. This is the electrodynamic basis of the Placidian equation.** Those who deny this measure in favor of that of Ptolemy must concede they are denying the fundamental facts of electrical science which have made possible the great modern advance in so many other branches of science. It would be absurd to suppose there is one set of electrical laws for a 60-cycle generator, another for radio, and a third to accommodate the immature notions of the followers of Ptolemy who have not yet grasped the fact that the invisible powers of the stars, Sun and planets are the electromagnetic waves, at light frequencies, which they respectively radiate and reflect to earth. The earth being a charged body at a potential of some seven millions of volts, moving with its accompanying electric and magnetic fields across the radial fields of the Sun and stars with a constantly changing inductive coupling with all these fields and with those of the other planets, which oscillate like quartz crystals at different lower (harmonic) frequencies proportionate to their masses and diameters†.

As the Midheavens in Table I are the **precessional** zeniths of the respective cities for 1930 for the time of the Sun's center on the vernal equinox, it follows that **the Placidian Solar arc for directing these Midheavens and Ascendants to**

---

† Consult Morecroft's text and works on piezo-electric crystals at to the effect of mass and diameter in determining the natural frequency of crystals.

the time of any eclipse or event of the year is simply the Sun's R. A. at the time of eclipse or event; the Sun's R. A. being zero at the ingress, for which the precessional cusps of the table are computed*.

To cite here a single example, let us assume we wish to know the annual progression of New York's precessional zenith for the time of the Solar eclipse, May 9th, 1929, in 18°07' Taurus. The solution follows:

(4)   315°09' RAMC New York 1930, Table I.
      — 01 Correction for 1929

      315°08' RAMC New York for 1929
      +45°39' R. A. Sun at eclipse in 18°07' ♉

(a)   360°47' Progressed M. C.
      360°00' Reject circle when (a) exceeds it

      0°47' R. A. = 0°51' ♈ M. C. of New York at eclipse.

From this M. C. the Ascendant would be found after the manner shown in Chapter III; or from a **Table of Houses** for New York latitude we may equate out the geographic Ascendant as about 19°32' Cancer.

Obviously, we may reverse the rule in order to determine the zenith or nadir longitude of a planet at the time of the eclipse. Where was Uranus at the eclipse zenith and nadir in the world horoscope in this progressed precessional sense? Solution:

      9°05' R. A. Uranus 9°36' Aries in lat. 0°41'S†
      360°00' Add circle in order to subtract arc

      369°05' R. A.
      —45°39' R. A. of eclipse.

      323°26' R. A. of place having Uranus at zenith at the eclipse

And,

---

* Another Solar arc must also be used, as will be explained presently.

† Any R. A. with latitude table, such as in Chaney's, Pearce's or Zadkiel's texts.

$$29°09'\ \text{R. A. Greenwich 1929, at ingress}$$
$$360°00'$$
$$\overline{389°09'}$$
$$-323°26'$$

65°43' West Long. Uranus on zenith
114°17' East Long. Uranus on nadir.

To find where a planet at eclipse, or the eclipse itself, is rising or setting in a given latitude, find the oblique ascension or descension of the planet or eclipse under the pole of the latitude.   Then if the latitude is **north** subtract 90° from the O. A. or add 90° to the O. D.; if the latitude is **south** add 90° to the O. A. or subtract 90° from the O. D.   From the remaining RAMC work out the solution as the last example will suggest.   It seems unnecessary to example this, as it will be familiar practice to those who have studied Chaney's or Pearce's texts, and the former is almost indispensable for rapid computation of oblique directions which do not involve planetary latitudes.   When the aspect is to be taken in celestial latitude, as is frequently the case, it is best to resort to trigonometry, as in many of the examples in the following chapters.

The distinction between the function of right ascensional and ecliptic conjunctions, or aspects, has been sketched in the author's text on the fixed stars, but for the guidance of those who may not possess a copy of that work, and because of the other facts which spring from it, it is necessary to restate the basic principle, viz.:

(a) The force across the **ecliptic** plane, as also across the planes of planetary latitudes parallel thereto, is **electromagnetic.**

(b) The force across the **equatorial or right ascensional plane,** as also across the planet's declination planes, or along the semiarcs, is **electrodynamic.**

In the former plane we measure the field strength, the static (voltage) induction, the psychological inducements, the "set of the pole pieces" of the cosmic generator. In the latter plane we measure the current flow, the flow of "current events," the "turn of events" or the commutative points.

But just as in a mechanical motor or generator, so in the cosmic machine—we may rotate (direct) the armature (the earth) in its right ascensional plane in the oblique (ecliptic) stationary field; that is, in the Sun's radial electric field and "across" its magnetic field, or we may rotate (direct) these latter fields about a stationary armature (earth); or we may, as in transformers, maintain a constant coupling (as when the planets are "stationary") and either fluctuate the current or reverse its direction, as when planets change their angular direction from direct to retrograde and vice versa. In all these ways a voltage and current change is induced because the celestial bodies are **charged** bodies. A change of energy or wattage results; and so as our English cousins would say: W'at now and w'at next?"—what events.

Now as regards the electrical interaction of the earth's, planets' and Sun's fields and motions, just what does this mean in a **directional** sense? It means there is **more** to the Placidian principle of directing than Placidus knew when he wisely forsook the Ptolemaic equation in favor of directing by the R. A. arc of the Sun as in equation (4) of this chapter, as in Chapter V, and in the (a) equations in Chapter VI. It means that just as **aspects** of planets and stars are valid **in** both the R. A. and longitudinal planes, as shown in the companion text, **so Solar directional arcs are valid in both R. A. and longitudinal units.**

The **ecliptic** or **longitudinal** arcs of the Sun's apparent motion measure the **shift of the Sun's electric field in the earth** in the plane of Fig. 2 and also **the shift of its magnetic field,** which is perpendicular thereto as shown by Figs. 5 and 6 in the text on the stars. The corresponding **R. A.** arcs of the Sun, known as the Placidian arcs, measure the **shift of the** "commutative" points of current events. **Neither measure can supplant the other. Both must be considered for any complete understanding of the manifestations of the Invisible Power.** For the one perpetual riddle of nations and individuals is weighing **the changing inducements** (ecliptic arcs) and trying to decide which among these many impulses will, if obeyed, **"turn out right"** (right ascensional arcs). Hence,

(c) When the problem is one of timing and qualifying the current event, the input or output in world affairs, use the Placidian arc—the R. A. arc of the Sun, as per equation (4).

(d) When it is a problem of timing and qualifying the pressure, demands, inducements or impulsions, use the Sun's longitudinal arc as follows: **Add to the precessional M. C. of the place the longitude of the sun from the vernal equinox. The sum is the longitude of the progressed M. C.** To example this, let us direct the New York zenith on the ecliptic arc for the time of the Solar eclipse, May 9th, 1929, in 18°07′ Taurus.

(5)   12°41′♒ M. C. New York 1930, Table I
       —· 01′   Correction to 1929
       ─────────
       12°40′♒ M. C.

       312°40′   Long. M. C. in ecliptic
        48°07′   Long. eclipse in 18°07′ ♉.
       ─────────
       360°47′
       360°00′   Reject circle
       ─────────
         0°47′♈ Long progressed M. C.

In **this** case the result differs only 5′ in longitude from the M. C. obtained by the R. A. arc as per (4). But for **some longitudes, and some times of the year, and some arc lengths,** the two equations may differ as much as about **six degrees,** and it would be a serious error to attempt to geographically locate the point of some great psychological wave of public sentiment or demand by employing the R. A. arc when the two equations so differ. Conversely, the place of a "current event" cannot be located by employing the ecliptic measure of the field force, except where they happen to agree in length. As a matter of fact a public or individual demand or urge may arise in one locality and cause "current events" to flow somewhere else.

While this complicates the riddle it is a condition in life and of the electromagnetic laws which we cannot escape, and it is no excuse to ignore the fact because it does not make astrology quite as simple as many of its believers wish it to be, nor nearly as simple as all its critics think it to be.

In a dynamo or motor the commutating brushes may be set a little ahead or behind the plane of the pole pieces†. If too much so there is a sputtering or sparking at the commutator. So, too, in the cosmic machine the Sun's R. A. arcs sometimes result in the Midheaven of a place "leading" the Midheaven as computed by the longitudinal arc, and sometimes "lagging" it. When the former is the case there is a current event followed by a psychological reaction in terms of an inducement or demand. In the latter case an individual or public demand arises and leads to the current event, and it is then said to be its cause instead of its effect. If the delay (arc difference) is maximum there is truly much sputtering or agitation about it. If the directions agree by both arcs, then it is one of those "psychological moments" when the subjective urges or the inducements and the objective events are "timely" with respect to each other.

It is because of these facts that we observe in one case, or at one time, that men make conditions. At another time conditions make or unmake the man. And still again, at some crucial moment, the man and the circumstance may appear

---

† In practice, ahead.

simultaneously.   Naturally this gearing of the Invisible Power
has led both wise and foolish minds into very antagonistic notions as to the question of freewill and determinism, with the
same sort of pointless testimonials on both sides as may be
accumulated for and against a patent medicine or any individual or sociological panacea.

Another point.   In all branches of astrology there is much
confusion among students as to the use of the direct and converse arcs.   While for simplicity the Solar arcs have been discussed and will be largely exampled as though they applied
only direct (eastward in zodiac), the reader is to understand
they also apply in the converse (westward) order. **The reason is to be found in the oscillatory nature of currents electromagnetically induced by light waves.**

Electrical laws here apply as in radio, with no difference
whatever except that the frequency is higher and the characteristics of low-frequency conductors and dielectrics are further reversed.   Those unfamiliar with electrical phenomena
may revert to the simpler, though imperfect, analogy of the
pendulum.   As long as the driving force is applied **the pendulum swings through equal opposite arcs in equal times; the
time** depending on the length (compare with wave length).
Electromagnetic waves radiate equally in opposite directions unless distorted or weakened by reflecting or absorbing mediums.
The inductions they set up are alternating. **At light frequencies
there is no sensible before or after in the timesense and no ap-
preciable before or behind in the spacesense**† Therefore the
use of direct and converse arcs of direction is not limited in
either case to pre-event and post-event concepts arising from
our **slow** timesense.

While it is beyond the scope of this text to stress or prove

† "On a body moving with the velocity of light length vanishes, becomes **zero,**
and the time stops"—Steinmetz's **Relativity and Space,** page 41.   See also
Chapter XI, **The Stars, How and Where They Influence.**

the need of sub-dividing the twelve "houses" (electric axes) of a figure on the one-sixth, one-half and five-sixth of the semi-arc, to conform to the more complete set of known electrical axes as revealed in crystals, it would be unfair to the broad-minded student and to the utility of this text not to cite a case as example. To this end the San Francisco earthquake will be cited in the next chapter. The correlative fact—that 15°, 75°, 105° and 165° are just as much "aspects" (electrical axes) as the better recognized angles†—will possibly appear in some of the examples.

Indeed there is in astrology so much in need of reform and extension that it is impossible to discuss any phase of the science from an electrical approach without doing violence here and there to the notions of copyists who in exalting the old masters decline to add to the science the fruits of recent researches in kindred fields.

Further rules of interpretation are omitted from this text, as they follow the same lines as those given in standard texts for the judging of aspects, elevations and house position; except that the aim should be to consider the **cuspal aspects** rather than resort to a mere desultory observation of the house placements of the planets. It may here be said, however, **that nothing startling should be too readily predicted from one testimony only.** It is advisable to check up the configurations of all eclipse figures of the year with the ingress or precessional cusps **and to direct for all the eclipses and ponderous stationaries, etc., as usually there will be found several important arcs bearing on the places of chief events.**

It is very essential that the investigator free his mind of the assumption that an eclipse must necessarily **precede** an event.

---

† Refer to works on molecular and atomic structures, crystallography and axes of rectifying and oscillating crystals.

Such is not the case at all†. Eclipses foreshadow striking events of the year, some before and some after the eclipse, according as the progressions and transits may excite the eclipse and planets' places thereat. The same holds true of other elective figures of the year, such as stationaries, great conjunctions, new moons, etc. As the author's text on the fixed stars explains how eclipses generate the current of events, and why they signify events which precede them as well as those which follow them, the reader should turn to that work to clear up this enigma. Ouspensky's **Tertium Organum** is recommended to those who would see beyond the illusions which bind the average consciousness to the wheel of time‡. See also preceding remarks on direct and converse arcs.

Before proceeding to instructive and verifying examples there is another technical consideration which must be made clear. In Chapter II it was stated the Sun's apparent diameter must be taken into account in the world horoscopes, just as in considering some directions in a nativity. As is well known, the Sun's disk subtends a geocentric angle of 32′. How this relates to the precessional cusps of Table I, and to their directions for the times of eclipse and events can best be explained by diagram.

Refer to the geocentric diagram, Fig. 3.

When the Sun is centered on the vernal equinox, at B, the Greenwich meridian is given in Table I as 1°19′ Taurus. But as the Sun radiates electromagnetic waves at light frequencies over a channel 32′ in width—beyond which they are weakened by deflection, or, as we say, by diffusion—these parallel radiations bombard the earth over a channel of equal width, with possibly more equal voltage amplitude over the whole

---

† See Pearce's quotation of Carden, page 323, his text.

‡ It is suggested the student make a careful study of Russell's **The A, B, C of Relativity**; Steinmetz's **Relativity and Space**; Tolman's **The Theory of the Relativity of Motion**; Eddington's **The Mathematical Theory of Relativity**, and works of similar nature.

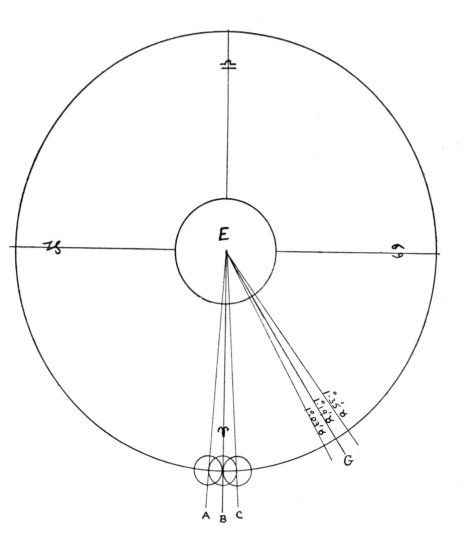

FIG. 3

channel than we have heretofore supposed; certainly much stronger than the deflected or diffused rays which spread out on both sides of this channel and illuminate half the earth with decreasing intensity towards the twilights of dawn and dusk. This is proven by the fact that the magnetic compass deviation from normal at a given station is greater at noon than at morning or evening.

When the Sun's **east** limb contacts the equinox* the Sun's center is at A, and the Greenwich meridian as explained in reference to Fig. 2 will be 1°19'—16', or 1°03' Taurus. When the Sun leaves the equinox, centering at C with its **west** limb contacting the equinox, the Greenwich meridian is 1°19'+16', or 1°35' Taurus. As the inductive transference at the equinox begins with the Sun at A, centers as maximum at B and passes off at C, it follows that since the Midheavens and Ascendants, as in Table I, are for the center, B, **there is a channel 16' east and west of each Midheaven within which events may be precipitated.**

Similarly the Ascendants in Table I are for the Sun at B, and they, as also the cadent and succeedent cusps, have a limiting arc or channel of influence within which major events may "crystallize" on either contact as well as when centered. The limiting arcs of the oblique cusps are more or less than 16' each way, depending on whether their motion is swift or slow as compared to the zenith motion.

Thus the Ascendant of London is 17°10' Leo, and there are 85'.5 O. A. in each ecliptic degree at that point in the latitude of London. Therefore the cusp limits become

$$\frac{16' \times 60'}{85'.5} = 11',$$

or from 16°59' to 17°21' Leo. As comparison the Ascendant of Los Angeles is 1°24' Aries. This point in latitude 34° has 39' O. A. in one degree, and the limits become

---

* The point of intersection of the two planes of the earth's motion as it moves and rotates as a charged body across the Sun's radial field.

$$\frac{16' \times 60'}{39} = 25',$$

or from 0°59′ to 1°49′ Aries.

For many practical purposes it suffices to allow a quarter-degree east and west of each cusp as calculated for the epoch, but it has seemed necessary to explain this point technically, otherwise the beginner would find some events argue the table's base should be a fraction of a degree farther east, while others would argue it should be a little farther west. Thus he might perhaps at once set about to revise in a moment, and without proper familiarity with the whole problem, what the author has taken twenty years to deduce after more consider-ations and misleads than a first reading of this treatise can respectively inspire and avert in the reader.

It seems to depend upon the general strength of the figure whether great events coincide with the limiting contacts or the center. Herein lies an unlimited field for further research; a field of rare delights for those of mathematical leaning and critically keen analysis.

In making tests of localities with **nativities**, after the man-ner in Chapter VI, it was repeatedly found by directing their "**birthday localities**" by the Solar arc, that the **west** limb con-tacts (C, Fig. 3) predominated at localities when the native left the place; **east** limb contacts (A, Fig. 3) when he approached a place for the first time or tarried casually and passed on; and central (B, Fig. 3) contacts at the places where he stayed to more importance. This is exactly what theory would antici-pate. There are exceptions, but thus far they are in the mi-nority.

It has been found in a very few cases that allowance must be made for the semi-diameter of the Sun both at the equinox and at the eclipse or event, making a disparity of 32′. It has also been noticed that there is more tendency, as a whole, **for events to center on one of the three contacts than on an arc**

mean between them. Indeed it was the repeated appearance of such inequalities as 16' of arc on the Midheavens, and their corresponding equivalents in the oblique sphere, that finally led to the consideration of the Sun's light channel or the arc of its disk. Much fruitless and disappointing quest might have been avoided had this fact and a better grasp of electromagnetic laws been earlier brought to bear upon the riddle.

Just as a radio-broadcast transmitter must have a carrier channel ten kilocycles in width to transmit the 5000-cycle high notes of music on each of its sidebands, so it **seems** the cusps and planets require a band the width of the Solar disk— its undeflected light channel—in which to function their "beat notes" upon the carrier wave of Solar light reflected by them to earth. Just what this statement means will be clearer to those who carefully study the companion text on the fixed stars.

It is quite within possibility, however, that a still more exhaustive research might reveal some overlooked technical consideration as would render void the present conclusion that the Sun's disk must be considered in the foregoing manner. It is far from the author's thought that this treatise is the last word on a subject which by its very nature involves and absorbs all other sciences.

Time may prove the semi-diameter of the Sun should be considered more often when the arc of direction is taken for an eclipse than when taken for the time of event, or when directing the BL figures for personal events as in Chapter VI. In some cases to which the solar disk **seems** to apply, a more searching investigation will show the apparent disparity to be due **to taking the direction in the field plane of the wrong planet, or to directing on the ecliptic (sine latitude) when the event is one pertaining to a planet's field rather than to the earth's.** As example see equation 2, example 6, Chapter V.

CHAPTER V

VERIFICATION BY WORLD EVENTS

Before presenting examples let us briefly sum up the most important principles which must be kept in mind in utilizing this text.

(1) Directions are effective in the ecliptic, in the parallel planes of the planets as defined by their latitudes, on the equator and along the parallel planes known as the planet's semi-arcs.

(2) Directional Solar arcs are effective both in R. A. and longitudinal units as defined by equations (4) and (5), Chapter IV, and as respectively applied to the RAMC and to the M. C. longitude of the place.

(3) All arcs are oscillatory and as such apply both direct and converse—clockwise and anti-clockwise.

(4) At light frequencies there is no such thing as a "before" or "after," and so eclipses and other electromagnetic inductive configurations signify events before as much as after them.

(5) It depends entirely on the nature of the event and on the celestial body most dominant at the eclipse or elective time, which planetary plane the electromagnetic coupling must be computed in.

(6) A direction between two celestial bodies or of the Midheaven or Ascendant to a planet may be taken in the field plane of a third planet when the event is colored by the characteristics of a planet other than those forming the mutual aspect.

(7) Direction of one eclipse, may be made to planets' places at the time of another eclipse preceding or following it by weeks or months or as much as a year, if not more.

(8) The mutual cross aspects existing between eclipses or elective figures are far more important than the mutual transits from day to day.

(9) The Sun's apparent semi-diameter needs consideration, at least in some cases where eclipses are directed.

(10) Each "house" of an astrological figure has a mid-angle (defined by the hour-angle) which should receive consideration*.

(11) All multiples of 15° are electrical axes or aspects, and thus 15°, 30°, 75°, 105° and 165° often bring about as significant events as those occurring on 45°, 60°, 90°, 120°, 135°, 150° and 180°.

(12) The use of geocentric or geographic latitude in computing arcs in the oblique sphere depends respectively upon the degree of "fatalism" and "volition' entering into the event —upon the objectivity or subjectivity of its cause or medium.

A few other considerations will appear with the examples, which will go far to show that "orbs of influence" are probably never necessary if we take the trouble to refer every direction to the plane consistent with the complete nature of the event†.

Unless the student will take up the use of this text with a mind open to all these principles he must expect to encounter

---

* It is largely the configurations to the hour-angles (electrical axes of the earth) that determine the crystallization or precipitation of "our" events. Many other words in our language have the same phonetic "sound sense" reaching back to the electro-mechanical and electromagnetic laws which give rise to the phenomena and to the concepts associated with words. Thus the Invisible Power is thinly veiled behind Man's vanity and conceit when he resorts to such common expressions as **"our** times," "in or out of **line,"** "out of my **latitude,"** "my **place in the world,"** "he is **right** or **righteous,"** they were **inclined** or **disinclined,"** and so on. Indeed, in recounting all his exploits or voicing his wrongs, vain man instinctively reverts to expressios which perpetually define the geometry and trigonometry of Einstein's "tangle of world lines" and the mutual inductions of their intersections.

† See **The Stars, How and Where They Influence,** Chapter X.

many events he cannot explain, or with which his computations do not very closely agree.

The events cited are chosen because they are familiar to
all, well scattered as to time and place and bring out some of
the most important of the foregoing points.

For simplicity something must be sacrificed in presenting
the examples. It would be tedious to superimpose explanation
upon explanation, and so some of the mathematical disparities
appearing in the examples must be passed over without the
comments they call for.   But here and there the apparent
mathematical errors or disagreements, such as due to citing
configurations in the familiar ecliptic plane, will be explained
away to the end of stimulating the student to think soundly in
terms of all these rather complex considerations, and particularly to induce him to consider the planetary latitudes in the proper way. More than this is impossible in so small a work on so
colossal a subject. Should an example appear obscure the
student should study the preceding chapters again and again.

That the reader entirely unfamiliar with the astronomical
symbols of the zodiacal signs may more readily understand the
application of the foregoing principles in this and the following
chapter, the signs are here listed opposite their symbols.

♈ Aries	♌ Leo	♐ Sagittarius
♉ Taurus	♍ Virgo	♑ Capricorn
♊ Gemini	♎ Libra	♒ Aquarius
♋ Cancer	♏ Scorpio	♓ Pisces

Wherever reference is made to electrical axes, or to the
equivalent astrological aspects of the Sun, Moon and planets,
the terms have the following meanings, the angle between these
bodies, or with respect to the Midheaven (zenith) or Ascendant (horizon), as the case may be, being referred to the
center of the earth.

Conjunction	0°	Square	90°
Semisextile	30°	Trine	120°
Semisquare	45°	Sesquiquadrate	135°
Sextile	60°	Quincunx	150°
	Opposition	180°	

Example 1. Let us take the great Chicago fire, October 8th, 1871, as a relatively simple case showing how Table I may often be studied with reference to such elective phenomena as ingress, eclipses, planetary stationaries, or major mutual aspects, with the minimum amount of directing. This may encourage beginners who imagine the technicalities of directing to be beyond their grasp.

The Chicago meridian for 1871 becomes

29°24′♑ M. C. for 1930, as per Table 1
—0°44′   Correction for 1871 (59 yrs. × 46″.10)
28°40′♑ M. C. for 1871.

At the ingress in 1871 the Moon was in 28°37′♓, in oppositon to Mars in 28°47′♍, thus in trines and sextiles with the upper and lower meridian of Chicago. At the ingress in 1870 Mars was in 28°17′♓, in square to Saturn in 28°17′ ♐. And so we may say the diminishing resultant induction of this coupling was reamplified by the superimposition upon it of the Lunar-Mars induction at the next ingress first cited. At the Solar eclipse, December 11th, 1871, Mars was in 26°37′♑, in opposition to Jupiter in 28°52′♋. Three days later there was a conjunction of the Moon with Mars in 28°37′♑ and an opposition of Mars in 28°40′♑ to Jupiter in 28°40′♋, Mars holding the Chicago zenith as above computed. If we direct this eclipse we have:

300°47′ R. A. of 28°40′♑, M. C. Chicago
258°50′ R. A. of Eclipse in 19°44′ ♐
———
559°37′
360°00′ Reject circle
199°37′ RAMC at eclipse
90°00′
———
289°37′ O. A.,

which in the latitude of Chicago, 41°54′N, gives the progressed Ascendant as 27°10′ ♐ , in close affliction with the cited
aspects at the two ingress figures and opposite the Solar
eclipse, June 17, 1871, in 26°24′♊†.

On August 9th, 1871, there was a square of Mars to
Uranus from 28°09′♎ and ♋, this being just the Sun's apparent diameter amiss from Chicago's lower meridian. On the
day of the fire Jupiter set off all these configurations by transiting the Chicago nadir.

All this shows how Mars' afflictions to large planets may
signify fire even when its rays do not occur at the time of an
eclipse. It also instructs the student that when two planets are
mutually adverse **even their trines or sextiles to locality angles
are to be read in terms of the mutual planetary aspect and not
in terms of their aspects to the earth angle or "house."**
This point must be constantly kept in mind. It is simply the
application of the ancient rule that "an afflicted planet can
accomplish no good"—even though in this case the fire was
touched off by the quite legitimate pursuit of milking a cow
that proved to be passing through the hasty and mean temper
of a Lunar opposition to Mars and a Mars square to Saturn,
which, occurring at the ingress times, seems to have spoiled
her springtime resolutions for the year, both as to 1870 and
1871.

It is seen an event is the product of a whole chain of interacting inductions or causes, and that we must consider the

† The disparity is due to directing on the ecliptic, sine latitude.

electromagnetic couplings which are set up over a spread of months, both in what our faulty timesense views as a 'before" and an "after." For this reason the reader should consider the words of Ptolemy: "But should it (a planet) be combined with others . . . . the coming event will then happen agreeably to the admixture and compound temperament* which arises from the whole communion† actually subsisting among the influencing powers. It would be a business of infinite labor and innumerable combinations quite beyond this treatise to set forth fully every contemperament and all configurations in every mode in which they can possibly exist, and knowledge of them must therefore be acquired by particular discrimination in every instance under the guidance of the precepts of science"‡.

This is so true that unfortunately no single set of rules can be given by which the student may glance at the table of locality angles and make predictions off hand from a single testimony as the novice may hope to do or as a thoughtless public expects the seasoned astrologer to do. The "tangle of world lines," though as orderly as the movements of the celestial bodies which give rise to their series, is so almost if not quite infinite in number, and the interacting waves so persistent— going on forever though in diminishing strength, that **there is no real beginning or end.** For practical purposes we are compelled to limit our considerations to the more immediate causes and major wave strengths centering within about a year around the event; both before and after, because the induced currents are alternating and involve the converse arcs as much as the direct, as will be illustrated in the next case.

Example 2. The Manila earthquake, June 3rd, 1863. This disaster was attended with a loss of about 10,000 lives.

---

* Resultant piezoelectric oscillation frequency.

† That is, from the sum of the electromagnetic field couplings and their phase relations.

‡ Particularly under the guidance of **electrical** laws.

Now if the student turns to Table I, reduces the Manila angles to 1863 and scans an 1863 ephemeris, after the manner of example 1, he is likely to be at a total loss to account for this event.

He should first refer back to the Lunar eclipse on June 12th, 1862, and note down that it occurred in 20°59′ ♐, in opposition to the longitude of Uranus' stationary, which followed in September in 20°45′♊, near the time of the autumn ingress. As may be gleaned from this case and that of the Tokio and Charleston earthquakes next cited, the worst earthquakes precede or follow the eclipses which configure Uranus. We can always view Uranus as a **voltage** amplifier, within the limitations of Neptune's "capacity effect" or supply; Saturn as either a "resistor" or a "step-down" transformer into a larger "current flow" (Jupiter)—or a larger flow of currency or fortune, for that matter.

Next we are to note that at the time of the Lunar eclipse on June 1st, 1863, two days before the earthquake, Uranus was in 20°16′♊. We must therefore couple the Manila locality with the 20th degree of Gemini*. The following calculation shows how this is done.

      150°08′ RAMC of Manila in 1930, Table I.
      —0°52′ Correction to 1863 (67 yrs. × 46″.10)
      149°16′ RAMC Manila in 1863
      —69°20′ R. A. Sun 10°55′♊, Lunar eclipse June 1, 1863.
        79°56′ R. A. = M. C. converse 20°45′♊

which we see is conjunction with Uranus' stationary in 20°45′♊ at the preceding autumn ingress. The arc is here

---

* Here the reader should note that at the battle of Manila Bay, later exampled, Neptune was in 20°46′♊. It refers to naval events as much as Uranus does to earthquakes. The reason this point of Gemini is a sensitive one in Manila's history, is to be found in the laws of the **fixed stars** as given in the author's companion text. Namely, star No. 1297, in mundo longitude 20°32′♊ in 1898 daily circled in latitude 14°07′S, geodetically nadir to Manila in 14°35′N. Also see No. 1346 which circles the latitude zenith of Manila and is in about this zodiacal longitude.

taken **converse** in the zodiac because we are directing a "later" eclipse to an "earlier" one, as our timesense at low frequency makes us view events in pulsating succession through our detection of but one sideband of the alternating light wave which, as it were, carries to us the word of God or the Invisible Power.

As another converse coupling we may direct the Manila Nadir converse for the preceding Solar eclipse on Dec. 6th, 1862, thus:

$$149°16' \text{ RAMC Manila 1863, as previous equation}$$
$$180°00'$$

$$\overline{329°16'} \text{ R. A. Nadir}$$
$$-252°38' \text{ R. A. Sun } 14°00' \text{ ♐ at Dec. 6th eclipse}$$

$$\overline{76°38'} \text{ R. A. Nadir converse } = \text{ Nadir } 17°42'\text{♊},$$

which is the exact longitude of Uranus on April 12th, 1863, when Mars transited the longitude of Uranus at the June 1st Lunar eclipse, near the conjunction of Mars and Uranus in 17°30'♊ on April 7th, 1863, near Uranus' stationary in 16°42'♊ in late February, and the trine of Jupiter in 17°41'♎ at the June 1st eclipse; Jupiter being then nearly geocentrically stationary.

If we direct the west limb of the Sun at the eclipse on June 1st, 1863, on the Solar arc of the eclipse on June 12th, 1862, we obtain the meridian of Manila in the world horoscope, thus:

(a) 69°03' R. A. west limb of Sun (center 10°55'♊—16')
(b) 80°11' R. A. Sun's center at eclipse June 12th, 1862.

$$\overline{149°14'} \text{ R. A., which is the RAMC of Manila for the epoch.}$$

Or we would obtain the same result if we direct the Sun's center for (a) on the arc of the Sun's west limb at (b). This illustrates the consideration of the Sun's semi-diameter.

Example 3. The Tokio earthquake, September 1st, 1923.

168°54' RAMC of Tokio in 1930, Table I
—0°05' Correction to 1923 (7 yrs. × 46".10)

168°49' RAMC 1923 = M. C. 17°50'℔.
180°00'

348°49' R. A. Tokio Nadir 1923.

The Solar eclipse on September 10th, 1923, occurred in 17°06'℔, near the Tokio ingress zenith in 17°50'℔, in opposition to Uranus in 15°30'♓ near the Tokio Nadir. In the text on the fixed stars† it is shown that this Tokio meridian eclipse in opposition to Uranus occurred with the eclipse and Uranus conjunction with two stars circling **latitudinally** Nadir to Tokio, to wit:

Star No. 24   zod. long. 15°46'♓ circling lat. 35°45'S
Star No. 2679   zod. long. 17°32'℔ circling lat. 35°40'S

The latitude of Tokio is 35°39'N (for the observatory there), and the companion text shows how this becomes a Nadir (in latitude) force, destructive to Tokio. **It is a splendid example showing how the two texts may be used together to determine the longitude and latitude where planetary forces are centered.** Yokohama, nearby, also suffered in this earthquake.

If this were the total evidence we would be very disappointed that the eclipse and Uranus did not closer satisfy the **longitudinal** equation. But we must observe that Uranus at the time of the summer solstice was stationary in 17°33'♓ and in latitude 0°47'S, the R. A. of this position being 348°53', which is just 4' (about as many miles) east of the above computed Nadir of Tokio, or nadir to Tokio Bay. Much loss resulted from the tidal wave which swept over the city with the shock. On the date of event Saturn transited 17°50'♎, the quincunx of the Tokio Nadir in 17°50'♓.

---

† Chapter VI, **Case 3.**

Directing Tokio for the event ,we find:

168°49′ RAMC Tokio in 1923
159°40′ R. A. Sun September 1st, 1923 (G. Noon)
328°29′ R. A.   =   M. C. 26°14′ ≈
 90°00′
 58°29′ O. A.

which under the **geocentric** latitude of Tokio, 35°28′N, gives
the progressed Ascendant in 17°05′♊, in square to the place
of the eclipse and Uranus' point of stationary. The progressed
Nadir would be 26°14′♌, and therefore on that day it passed
the place of Mars 26°27′♌ at the Lunar eclipse on August
26th, 1923.   Great destruction to property (Nadir or 4th
house) resulted from the fire (Mars) which swept the city
following the shock and tidal wave. This was also indicated
by directing the Solar eclipse thus:

168°49′ RAMC Tokio in 1923
168°08′ R. A. of Solar eclipse in 17°06′♍
336°57′ R. A. = M. C. 5°07′♓,

which is a close opposition to Mars on the Nadir in 6°16′♍ at
the time of the eclipse.

We may go further back to the Solar eclipse on March
17th, 1923, in 25°55′♓, and find the progressed Tokio Nadir
was at that time in R. A. 345°05′, in mundo conjunction with
Uranus then in 14°15′♓ with 0°44′S latitude, the R. A. of the
planet being therefore 345°13′.

Here again the **extent** of the disaster is to be read from
the **number** of concurrent field couplings found at the place
when **all** the principal celestial phenomena — eclipses, great
stationaries and major aspects—causing great changes in the
earth's field force and eddy currents are considered. The student must not become a public alarmist because or when he
finds but one powerful coupling of an eclipse with a certain
locality. The great disasters are the result of the sum of sev-

eral superimpositions of electric fields in the planes of particularly such electrical axes as the opposition and square However, for many of the minor events which daily fill the public press, one coupling is often all that is necessary or easily found to account for it.

The mathematics of this text are like those of Kepler's law and many other fundamental equations, absurdly simple, and should be mastered by the average reader in a few hours. But only long practice can develop good judgment in tracing out the evidence as related to the many kinds of events, or become a safe guide to predictive judgment for those who aspire to the role of prophet rather than to a scientific and philosophic understanding of the world in which we live and of those worlds about us which we now see are there not only "for signs and for seasons," but for **cause** — to work the Master's will in the Cosmic Body within which we move and have our being.

If to shortsighted mortals it appears cruel that the Invisible Power should induce wars and earthquakes as well as, for us, more agreeable events, let them question whether a good man is any less noble because the microscope and the test tube today tell us he owes his existence as much to the destruction of millions of cell life daily as to the birth of still other millions of cells .

In a universe in which life depends on service in an ascending series, the business of man as an executive and as a behavorist is not to make war on the "lower life" for the sake of the "higher life," nor vice versa, but rather through the extension of his co-operativeness make and keep his peace with all life in the series. Meaning what he "detects" in life is that to which he attunes himself. If he cannot or will not attune himself to a desirable program, or fails to find a place in life or in the world wherein he can express the best "plan its" that influence him, he must not blame the Invisible Power for his loss, accident or sickness. Calamity overtakes only those who are in some respect **out of tune and out of place.** The best proof of this is that in practically all great catastrophies **some** of those involved escape—**the rest are in greater or less degree misfits.** These life and society in any plane of the series must inevitably either reform by replacement or, failing therein, by divers ways eliminate.

Example 4. The Charleston, S. C., earthquake, August 31st, 1886.

Briefing this case it will be found from Table I that the Charleston M. C. in 1886 was 6°23′♒. Subtracting the Sun's semidiameter of 16′ we obtain 6°07′♒ as the M. C. for the Sun's east limb contact with the equinox. On August 29th, 1886, two days before the event, there was a Solar eclipse in 6°04′♍, quincunx with the M. C. At this eclipse Uranus was 6°07′♎ in trine to the M. C.†, thus coupling the earlier square of Uranus to Saturn with that longitude. On the day of the earthquake Mars transited 6°♏, in sextile to the place of the eclipse and in square to the Charleston M. C. and Nadir. Directing for the eclipse brings the M. C. 15°19′♋, which is the trine of the solar eclipse on March 5th, 1886, in 15°17′♓; Mars being then opposite the eclipse in 16°07′♍.

Directing the Charleston Ascendant for the latter eclipse gives 6°31′♉, which is the trine of the August eclipse, the quincunx of Uranus then in 6°33′♎, the square of the city's precessional zenith and the opposition of Mars on the day of the event. The companion text shows how certain fixed stars defined the **latitude** of this event by configuring the eclipse, Uranus and Mars.

Example 5. The San Francisco earthquake, April 18th, 1906.

---

† The R. A. of Uranus in latitude 0°40′N was 185°52′. Taken on the ecliptic this R. A. gives 6°23′♎, trine to the Charleston M. C.

This disaster is cited not only because of the remarkable latitudinal coupling shown in the text on the fixed stars, but as an example of a configuration with what for distinction may be designated as a sub-cusp—an hour-angle dividing the two-hour division termed a "house". This is in accord with the author's practice of viewing every hour-angle (15°) as an aspect. The reason is to be found in the electrical characteristics of crystals as defined by crystallography, by their self-oscillation characteristics in high-frequency vacuum-tube circuits and by their various lines of fracture when crystals are cracked by excessive oscillation under high voltage impressed upon them at their natural frequencies.

In this case it is desired to show the planetary couplings with the middle of the 10th house, or the first ecliptic hour-angle east of the M. C. Computing the M. C. for 1906, we have:

```
266°46'  RAMC San Francisco in 1930, Table I
—0°19'   Correction to 1906 (24 yrs. × 46".10)
266°27'  RAMC in 1906
 15°00'  One hour-angle
281°27'  O. A. of mid-10th.
```

This under the pole (7°27') of the angle gives the mid-10th as 7°34'♑.

The polar elevation of the first hour-angle east or west of the Midheaven or nadir may be found in the usual way given in standard texts for computing the pole of a house, except that as 15° is one-sixth of a quadrant you must take one-sixth of the ascensional difference instead of one-third as for the 11th and 3rd house, and so on. If we look in a **Table of Houses** for the approximate latitude of San Francisco, we will see that when 27° ♐ is on the M. C. 19°♑ is the cusp of the 11th house. The 10th house is therefore 22° in length. Half this added to the M. C. gives 8°♑. As the M. C. is not actually

27° ♐ , but a little less, we know by inspection that the mid-
10th is about 7½°♑. We may then find the true pole as
follows:

7½°♑ in declination	23°15′	tangent	9.633099
Geocentric latitude	37°36′	tangent	9.886549
A. D.	19°19′	sine	9.519648

and,

One-sixth A. D.	3°13′	sine	8.749055
Declination	23°15′	cotan.	0.366901
Pole of mid-10th	7°27′	tangent	9.115956

Proving this, we have

R. A. of 7°34′♑	278°14′
A. D.	3°13′
O. A. required	281°27′,

which is the O. A. of the San Francisco mid-10th for 1906,
as computed from Table I by preceding equation.

Now what do we find configuring 7°34′♑ at the elective
times of 1906? The answer may be tabulated thus:

Uranus conjunction in	7°30′♑ at eclipse February 23
Neptune opposition in	7°37′♋ at ingress.
Mercury st. square in	7°33′♈ at event
Mars opposite in	7°01′♋ at summer solstice.
Mars square Neptune in	7°53′♈ and ♋ February 15.
Mars square Uranus	7°07′♈ and ♑ February 14.
Mean of last two	7°30′♑
Uranus stationary in	8°29′♑ at event.

An as exercise in directing, the student should check up the
following additional features. Directing the San Francisco
Ascendant for geocentric latitude for the time of the shocks
gives it as 4°40′ ♉ , which is the **exact** longitude of Mars at the
first new moon closely following the ingress. Directing for
the Solar eclipse on February 23rd, 1906, brings the Midheaven close square to that eclipse. Directing for the Lunar
eclipse on Feb. 9th, 1906, brings the Midheaven semisquare to

Uranus at that eclipse and the Nadir close to the place of Mars at the disaster. Directing for the time of Mars (fire) square to Uranus (quake), when the Sun was in 24°51′♒, brings the Nadir 25°55′♉, over which Mars transited while fire swept the city during the four days following the shocks. There are other factors, and for simplicity the converse directions have been omitted in this and the preceding example.

Example 6. The sinking of the Maine, Feb. 15th, 1898.

306°48′ RAMC Havana in 1930, Table I
—0°25′ Correction to 1898
306°23′ R. A. = M. C. 4°03′♒

The Solar eclipse on January 22nd, 1898, occurred in 2°08′♒, conjunction with the M. C.†, in sextile to Uranus (explosions) and sesquiquadrate to Neptune (ships). On the day of the event Mars transited 4°♒, over the zenith. War (Mars) grew out of the event.

It should be noted that the Solar eclipse on July 29th, 1897, was in 6°44′♌, and that the mean opposition of this eclipse and the later one in 2°08′♒ becomes

$$\frac{2°8' + 6°44'}{2} = 4°26'♒ \text{ and } ♌,$$

nearly the Havana meridian*.

† For those who wish to investigate the importance of the fact that the earth's magnetic field deviates in most places more or less from the right ascensional meridian, it may be useful to here observe that the magnetic declination at Havana in 1898 was 3°05′ east of north. The astronomic declination of 4°03′♒ (the M. C. as above) is 19°16′S, and the geocentric latitude of Havana is 23°01′N. From these elements it is easy for those versed in trigonometry to compute that the magnetic meridian of Havana was about 2°02′♒, conjunction with this eclipse. When the magnetic deflection is small, as in this case, the true solution, which is more tedious, is very closely given by

19°16′+23°01′ = 42°17′ sine 9.827884
3°05′ tan. 8.731317
2°05′ tan. 8.559201

And 306°23′— 2°05′ = 304°18′ R. A. = 2°02′♒, magnetic meridian of Havana.

* See example 11 on **equatorial** couplings.

Directing Havana on the Sun's arc for the event, we find the M. C. to be $5°18'\text{VS}$, a day's motion past the place of Mars in $4°22'\text{VS}$ at the Lunar eclipse on January 7th, 1898. This also was an indication war would follow. Directing Washington for this eclipse, we have

312°10′ RAMC Washington, Table I
—0°25′ Correction to 1898
——————
311°45′
(a) 289°17′ R. A. Sun 17°48′VS at this eclipse
——————
601°02′
360°00′ Reject circle
——————
241°02′ Prog. R. A. = M. C. 3°05′ ♐

At the time of the event Uranus was in $3°22'$ ♐. Had we directed the east limb of the Sun at this eclipse, instead of its center, this co-ordination would be exact. For $17°48' + 16'$ (angular semidiameter of Sun) is $18°04'\text{VS}$, in R. A. 289°35′ in lieu of (a), from which the above equation gives the M. C. as $3°22'$ ♐ †.   Refer to preceding comments on the Sun's disk.

We may direct Madrid for this Lunar eclipse and find its progressed Ascendant for the geocentric latitude to be $5°34'\text{II}$, and note that Mars passed this point on the day the American forces invaded Porto Rico, and that Saturn was **stationary** opposite this point in $5°39'$ ♐ at the end of the war August 12-13th, 1898.

For the indications of the battle of Manila Bay, May 1st, 1898, we find the following instructive couplings:

150°08′ RAMC Manila 1930, Table I
—0°25′ Correction to 1898
——————
149°43′
304°24′ R. A. eclipse in 2°08′≈
——————
454°07′
360°00′ Reject circle
——————
94°07′ R. A.   =   M. C. 3°46′♋ and Asc. 4°02′♎

---

† The M. C. was conjunction with Uranus **in the plane of Mars.** As war followed, this is the more logical solution and does not involve the Sun's semidiameter.

Thus Mars in 4°22′♑ at the Lunar eclipse on Jan. 7th, was on the progressed Nadir of Manila Bay and square to the Ascendant.
And,

149°43′ RAMC at ingress as above.
 38°40′ R. A. Sun (G. N.) on day of battle
─────
188°23′ RAMC
 90°00′
─────
278°23′ O. A.,

which in the geocentric latitude of Manila, 14°30′N, gives its progressed Ascendant 1°47′♑, square to Mars 2°♈ on that date. Mars being then sextile to the place of the January eclipse. Mars was then also in R. A. conjunction with star No. 27, Boss Catalogue, as the star's R. A. then intersected the ecliptic in 2°11′♈. It circled daily in geographic latitude 14°42′N, nearly latitudinally zenith to Manila in 14°36′N; thus co-ordinating Mars with that latitude in the manner shown by C, Figs. 1 and 2 in the text on the stars. This is a good example of the joint utility of the principles of the two texts, as obviously the place of events can be determined only by solving both the longitudinal and latitudinal field couplings at the same time.

In this manner it is possible to check up every center directly involved in any war and to time and place the various major incidents of the drama. Obviously, however, to do so in connection with any one war is a prolonged labor and would fill a volume.

One very important thing that the limited number of examples possible in this text show, is that **the electrical axes of a locality are to be rotated or directed on the Solar arc of the eclipse or elective figure to the places of planets at other eclipses and elective times during the year.** The coupling of one eclipse with another in this manner is of even more significance than directing an eclipse to a planet's place at that

eclipse, not that the latter is to be neglected. Why this is so
is easy to see from an electrical point of view when we consider that an eclipse, a planetary stationary, etc., causes a
change in mutual induction between the celestial bodies, a
change in the earth's field strength and a change in its eddy
currents which is the cause not only of earthquakes, but also,
together with the more direct inductions from light waves, the
source from which living organisms draw their motive power.
That is why it is useless for science to seek the **source** of life
in the biologic cell or in the food we eat, and why the physi-
cian's specific fails on the patient whose current source is cut
off by an eclipse under certain phases of its electromagnetic
couplings with the planets in the patient's nativity.

Fortunately the invention of the oscillating vacuum tube
has now turned the eyes of science in the right direction for an
understanding of the mysteries of life and death. Or at least
will have done so when **it is seen that our Solar System is a
self-contained, self-oscillating system in a constant state of inductive variance with respect to the electric and magnetic fields
of the charged masses which compose it.** Had electrical laws,
as we know them today, been known in Newton's or Kepler's
time they at least would have seen that this is so. Einstein's
identification of magnetism and gravitation as one law will
shortly make this clear to science.

It is the shame of Science that, knowing what it knows today, it is in this sense wasting its data in ever narrowing spe-
cializations which, however admirable to the advancement of
artificialities, bring it no nearer a comprehension of the Invisible Power which guides the whole.

Example 7. The Declaration of Independence.

Let us now show that Uranus was exactly on the 11th
angle of London on July 4th, 1776. The 11th angle has long
been attributed by many astrologers as the "ruler" of parlia-

ment, and Uranus is invariably tied in with revolutions.

> 29°02′ R. A. London† 1930, Table I.
> —1°58′ Correction to 1776 (154 yrs. × 46″.10)
> (b) 27°04′ RAMC London in 1776
> 30°00′
> 57°04′ O. A. of 11th angle

At this event Uranus was in 8°51′♊, in declination 21°47′N*. Hence its oblique ascension under the polar elevation of the 11th angle in the latitude of London becomes

Declination	21°47′	tangent	9.601663
Latitude	51°32′	tangent	0.099913
Asc. Diff.	30°12′	sine	9.701576

1/3 Asc. Diff.   10°04′ for 11th angle

and,

> R. A. of 8.51♊ is 67°08′‡
> A. D. of 8.51♊ is 10°04′
> O. A.   Uranus   57°04′,

which agrees with the O. A. of London's 11th angle for 1776 as just computed. The **geographic** latitude of London is taken because the event is Uranian and man-made, and rose out of the attitude of the British parliament towards the American colonists**.

Coupling the position of Uranus, the revolutionist, with the American phase of this famous document, it is easy to compute from Table I that Boston's geographic and geocentric Ascendants were 9°16′ and 9°06′♊, the latter just the solar semi-diameter from conjunction with Uranus. In other words, the line of Uranus on the Ascendant passed a little west of Boston, **through Concord.** Uranus on the Ascendant means a

---

† For the longitude of the Parliament Buildings.
* See Weston's **Astrolite on the Presidents.**
‡ Uranus being close to its node its R. A. is taken on ecliptic sine latitude.
** Referring to the Navigation Acts, the Sugar Act, the Stamp Act, the Coercive Act and the **Tea Act.**

people in revolt*. The Declaration thus at that crucial moment grew out of Britain's preceding legislative acts and the resulting resentment of the Massachusetts colony which focused the de-cisive spark at Bunker Hill, Concord and Lexington in 1775. Uranus was in close trine to the meridian of Philadelphia where the document was signed and, of course, trine to the bay ports to the south, whose shippers, like those of Boston and New York, were most directly hit by the mother country's legislative enactments. If we direct the Eastern-American zenith to July 4th, 1776, we find Uranus was then in the Mid-heaven, pointing to successful (M. C.) revolution (Uranus). At London the Midheaven passed the exact sextile of Uranus on that day, thus:

> 27°04′ R. A. London in 1776 (see (b) equation)
> 104°21′ R. A. Sun at reputed time of signing
> _____
> 131°25′ R. A. ⚌ M. C. 8°59′♌, sextile Uranus 8°51′♊

The couplings in latitude will be found in the other text.

Example 8. The Civil War, April 12, 1861.

Referring briefly to the Revolution, it may be said it offers the student of world affairs a splendid set of exercises in the use of this text. He should first note that Uranus was again transiting the Ascendants of Eastern America and in trine to the Midheavens of Washington and adjacent States. He should then compute the Midheavens of Ft. Sumter and Ft. Moultrie for that epoch and find them to be 5°59′ and 6°03′♒; noting that the Lunar eclipse on January 26th, 1861, occurred with the Sun and Moon respectively on their upper and lower meridian in 6°45′♒ and ♌, and that Mars, transit-ing the Eastern Ascendants, passed the sextile and trine of

<hr>

* This ray repeated in 1861, and will bring a third American crisis not later than 1945 and possibly as early as 1942 not merely as between America and Britain but as between the industrial and agricultural blocks in America—the former's need of an ever-widening friendly market abroad, the latter's need of more drastic tariff protection at home, by that time an irreconcilable issue as regards keeping the peace at home or jeopardizing it to keep it abroad.

these points from 6°♊ on April 12th and 13th, 1861, when war began with opening fire between the forts; the Moon joining with Mars on the 13th when fire swept Ft. Sumter and forced Major Anderson's abandonment of it†. Here the student may also note that the Moon transited the Charleston meridian on February 8th, 1861, when the Provisional Government under Davis was established there.

Next he would compute the Midheaven of Bull Run and find it then in 8°19′♒. This is just the solar semi-diameter from the trine of Uranus' stationary in February when the Confederate government was set up; it is also practically the point of mean opposition of the Lunar eclipse of Jan. 26th, 1861, in 6°45′♌, and the Lunar eclipse of August 1st, 1860, in 9°34′♒, and Mars excited these points by transiting 10°♌ on the date of battle, July 21st, 1861, this transit coupling with the eclipses and the meridian of the place during the few preceding days of preparation. Obviously, for a complete picture, all the eclipses for a year or two before the war, and all those occurring during the long struggle, must be taken into consideration. Each of them relates to certain phases (electromagnetic phases) of the war. For instance, on the opening day of the war Mars was exactly on the progressed Nadir of Washington for the Solar eclipse on Jan. 11th, 1861. As a result, the first act of war (Mars) was committed by the South against (opposite) the government (M. C.). This blunder on the part of the South, and which Davis had sought to avoid, gave Lincoln a united North, less certain of easy accomplishment had the first overt act been on the side of the government.

Example 9. The Great War, 1914-1918.

It is shown in the author's text on the fixed stars that the Solar eclipse on August 21st, 1914, in 27°35′♌, casting its

---

† Compare with Example 4 for same location.

shadow across Europe, is the key to the war; not only for the
reasons we will see presently, but because it occurred in the
longitude of Mars, $27°44'\Omega$, at the summer solstice, and because the armistice came within a few hours of the time Saturn arrived at the longitude of this eclipse after transiting two
full signs during the war, it being sextile to the place of the
eclipse on and around July 30th, 1914. Let astrological critics
compute for themselves, from the slow angular velocity of this
thirty-year wanderer, moving an average of about 2' of arc a
day, how poor an argument is their uninformed cry—"coincidence!"

From Table I, reduced to 1914, we may readily see that
this eclipse not only cast its shadow over Europe and set up
the currents of war fever as shown by Fig. 7 in the companion
text, but that it also occurred on the precessional Ascendants
of Europe along an oblique line joining Berlin, Vienna and
the Aegean. In war computations the Ascendants are usually
to be taken for the **geographic** latitude; because war is the act
of man, and so we must consider the spheroidal distortion of
the field force in him as in any organic or gaseous bodies.
Taking the Berlin and Vienna Ascendants for 1914, in the
ecliptic plane, we find them respectively $27°00'$ and $27°17'\Omega$.

Now if we were to "let it go at that" the student would be
disappointed that these do not quite coincide with the place
of the eclipse, and the critic would sit comfortably back with
another murmured "coincidence" and go his characteristically
indolent way in righteous self-conviction that his murmur is
the very essence of science.

To stay these equally unwarranted reactions the reader
must be mindful of the instructions which precede these examples. He must see that as Austria served the first ultimatum
and declaration of war we must electromagnetically link the
Vienna Ascendant with the eclipse, not in the earth's plane
(ecliptic), **but in the plane of Mars,** whose field threaded the

earth in a parallel plane a little north of the ecliptic. Let us test this as follows:

45°30' RAMC Vienna in 1930, Table I.
—0°12' Correction to 1914 (16 yrs. × 46".10)
45°18' RAMC in 1914
90°00'
135°18' O. A. Vienna Ascendant in 1914.

As at the time of the eclipse Mars was in 0°29'N latitude, we have:

27°35'♌ in 0°29'N lattiude = Dec. 12°46'N
27°35'♌ in 0°29'N latitude = R. A. 149°58'

and,

Declination	12°46'	tangent	9.355227
Lat. Vienna	48°14'	tangent	0.049121
Asc. Diff.	14°42'	sine	9.404348

and,

R. A.   149°58'
A. D. —14°42'
O. A.   135°16'.

This is so nearly in accord with the above O. A. as to fall within the city limits, within two miles of the point used to compute the city in Table I.

Now Berlin. As rightly or wrongly chief responsibility for this dark blot (eclipse) upon civilization has been saddled upon Germany, as at that time the faithful disciple of her alleged mad Kaiser, and as the Moon was the body casting the shadow and is attributed to unbalanced natures, let us see if the Moon at the eclipse was centered on Berlin's Ascendant more nearly than was the Sun. That is, let us see if it was at Berlin that mere good or bad **sense** (Moon) cut off the brighter beams of **wisdom** (the Sun).

The Moon at the eclipse was in 0°46′N latitude.
Hence,

$$27°35′\,\Omega \text{ in } 0°46′N \;=\; \text{Dec. } 13°02′N$$
$$27°35′\,\Omega \text{ in } 0°46′N \;=\; \text{R. A. } 150°04′$$

and,

Declination	13°02′	tangent	9.364515
Lat. Berlin	52°31′	tangent	0.115281
Asc. Diff.	17°34′	sine	9.479796

and,

R. A.   150°04′
A. D. --17°34′

O. A.   132°30′ Required for Moon on Ascendant

Computing Berlin, we have:

42°34′ RAMC Berlin in 1930, Table I
—0°12′ Correction to 1914
42°22′ RAMC in 1914
90°00′
132°22′ O. A. Berlin's Ascendant.

This is about eight miles amiss of exact co-ordination. In Table I Berlin is computed for the longitude and latitude of **the observatory** there and of course this is not the exact point of reference for political and national issues. The distance and direction of the Palace and Government Buildings from the observatory has not at this writing been ascertained by the author. Part of the error may be in the interpolative tables used in computing the latitude of the Moon, its declination and right ascension. The error is small considering the size of the city.

Moreover, we must not forget that at the time of the summer solstice Mars was in 27°44′ Ω and in latitude 1°11′N. The oblique ascension of this point, under the geographic latitude of Berlin, works out as 132°18′, or about four miles west

of the Ascendant for the observatory location there.   Here
we see Berlin was truly the stage of the rising war lord.

While it would be absurd to say the assassination of Arch-
duke Ferdinand, on June 28th, 1914, at Sarajevo (Seraieva),
was the **cause** of the war, it is plain this event became the
excuse for conflict over an intolerable condition in the Balkans
arising out of the Balkan wars and the Bosnia affair.   For
Sarajevo, we have:

> 28°58′ RAMC Greenwich reduced to 1914 from Table I
> 18°26′ Longitude of Sarajevo East*
> $\overline{}$
> 47°24′ RAMC in 1914
> 90°00′
> $\overline{}$
> 137°24′ O. A. in latiutde 45°54′N* gives Asc. 27°23′ ♌.

This is within 12′ of conjunction with the eclipse†.   But
as the assassination was a Mars event and the harbinger of the
war, we should here also as in the case of Vienna compute the
Ascendant conjunction with the eclipse **in the plane of Mars.**
Testing this we obtain O. A. 137°22′, which is but 2′ amiss;
as near as to be expected when scaling a city from a small map.
It is unnecessary to show the calculation.   Simply substitute
the latitude of Sarajevo for that of Vienna and proceed as in
that equation.

Now let us direct Sarajevo's Ascendant on the Solar arc
of the eclipse.

> 47°24′ RAMC Sarajevo in 1914, as computed above
> 149°47′ R. A. of eclipse in 27°35′ ♌.
> $\overline{}$
> 197°11′ R. A.
> 90°00′
> $\overline{}$
> 287°11′ O. A. in latitude 43°42′N gives Ascendant 23°37′ ♐

Saturn transited the exact opposition of this point,
23°37′♊, on the day of the assassination so fraught with fa-

---

* Approximately scaled from map.

† The latitudinal coupling of eclipse with Sarajevo and Belgrade will be found
in Chapter **XI**, **The Stars, How and Where They Influence.**

talistic (Saturn) consequences to the world. Here the direction is taken in **geocentric** latitude because the coupling is
with Saturn, as explained in Chapter II. It is true the deed
was committed "in the form of a man," but we may always
view a man under the influence of Saturn as very much
"possessed by the devil" and stupidly irresponsible as to his
inner motives however dependable to carry out an **objective**
task. Through such natures the "devil is loosened" to roam
the earth‡. As earlier stated, it is generally necessary to use
geocentric latitude where the oblique sphere relates to this
planet.

Without making this example too tedious it may be stated,
without tabulating the calculations, that Berlin's Midheaven
for this eclipse was conjunction with Mars in 13°29′≏ at the
time of the Lunar eclipse on September 4th, 1914; **precisely**
so if, as we should, we compute this coupling **in the plane of
Uranus** at the Lunar eclipse. For the R. A. of Mars in
13°29′≏, in the latitude of Uranus then 0°40′S, was 192°08′,
and the R. A. of the Solar eclipse added to the Berlin M. C.
gives 192°09′ R. A. This coupling is taken in the field of
Uranus because of the Emperor's dictatorial (Uranian) stand
in the war (Mars) crisis.

Though America did not enter the war until April 1917,
it is instructive to note that when on April 9th, 1917, we de-
clared war on Austria—the first declarant of war in the 1914
crisis—the Washington meridian was in line with the place
of the eclipse, thus:

312°10′ RAMC Washington 1930, Table I
—0°10′ Correction to 1917
312°00′ RAMC in 1914
17°47′ R. A. Sun 19°16′♈, Apr. 9, 1917, Washington noon.
329°47′ R. A. = M. C. 27°35′♒.

---

‡   Saturn, like any planet, is "evil" only in its **lunar** (reversal) phase.

This is opposite the eclipse in 27°35′♌. In other words, the Washington **Nadir** was conjunction with the eclipse, and America came in to help **end** (nadir effect) the war. This shows that a current change induced by an eclipse often enters into current events for two or more years. Electrically speaking, an eclipse superimposes a localized (shadow path) "damped wave train" upon the ordinarily undamped solar waves†. The effect of such a wave train, or its passing and the restoration to the normal undamped rhythm, is thus seen to be slow. This is why the early astrologers were not wholly amiss in declaring the effects of an eclipse to last as many years as the eclipse contact measures in hours.

Space will not permit showing more of the inductive couplings at the various capitals of all the nations involved. They constitute an interesting study which the student should not pass over if he hopes to master the application of this text in all its ramifications. However, at the time of this Solar eclipse Mars was in 4°23′♎, and the reader who has no intention of making a personal study of astrology will be interested to know where Mars was at the zenith at this eclipse according to the progression of the precessional dial at that time. The solution is very simple, as follows:

$$
\begin{aligned}
184°12′ &\text{ R. A. of Mars in } 4°23′♎, \text{ in latitude } 0°29′\text{N} \\
-149°47′ &\text{ R. A. of eclipse in } 27°35′♌ \\
\hline
34°25′ &\text{ R. A., or terrestrial longitude east of equinox} \\
-28°58′ &\text{ R. A. Greenwich in 1914 reduced from Table I} \\
\hline
5°27′ &\text{ R. A., or } \textbf{East Longitude}
\end{aligned}
$$

On a map of Europe the reader will see this longitude approximates the western battlefront where centered the decisive struggle of the war. The line should also be taken as computed on the ecliptic and in the field planes of **all the other planets**, thereby covering the irregularities of the battle lines.

---

† For characteristics of damped and undamped waves, see Bureau of Standards circular No. 74, or Morecroft's **Principles of Radio Communication.**

Thus the god of Might (Mars), for four years (Mars 4°) hanging in the balance (sign Libra), trampled Northeastern France and Belgium into a shamble, till Saturn with its Hymn of Hate, mutual distrust and national fears, arrived at the longitude of the eclipse on November 11th, 1918, saw, so to speak, the dark picture Central Europe's moon-madness had produced, and became, as Saturn ("Satan") eventually always must, the quitter.

Those studying the text on the fixed stars will find it instructive to look up in the Boss catalogue the declinations* of stars mundo and zodiacal conjunction with this position of Mars. They will find, for instance, that in 1914 star No. 2503, circling close to the geodetic nadir of Petrograd, in the latitudinal sense, was in zodiacal longitude 4°03′≏; No. 2674 was in 4°40′≏ and in like geodetic relation to Germany; while No. 3176 and No. 3163 were in close mundo conjunction with Mars and respectively circling geodetically opposite England and France, near the oppositions of London and Paris.

On a map we may easily project the line of Ascendant sextile to Mars at this eclipse and find it passed slightly east of London and across the Channel on a line with Nantes; thus putting the Tight Little Isle just west of the fields of carnage.

If we turn to the eastern front we will see from Table I that the eclipse not only centered on the Ascendant along a line from Berlin to the Aegean—the Central Powers line of desired penetration southeastward to the sea—but that it was also square to the zenith in meridian 26°21′ East, over which the eastern tides of war ebbed and flowed, and which later became the center of the buffer states Esthonia, Latvia and Lithuania and the border dividing Poland from Russia and Ukraine. Incidentally, these are closely the Ascendants and Midheavens coupled with the Kaiser's Uranus, and over which the division

---

* Corrected to geographic-latitude equivalents by Table II of the present text.

(Uranus) of interests arose with the paramount question as to who would be supreme czar (Uranus) along these territorial lines.

Example 10. The Titanic disaster, April 14th, 1912, in 50°15′W and 41°46′N (collision).

```
29°10′ RAMC Greenwich in 1930
—0°14′ Correction to 1912
28°56′ RAMC 1912. (Add circle to subtract)
—50°15′ Longitude West
338°41′ R. A.   =  M. C.  6°57′♓.
```

This is trine to Mars in 6°35′♋ at the Solar eclipse on April 17th, 1912; the sesquiquadrate to Neptune in 21°04′♋ at the same Solar eclipse and the conjunction of Mars in 5°43′♓ at the opposition of Jupiter and Saturn just following the Solar eclipse of April 28th, 1911. .The usual disparity arises from referring all these aspects to the ecliptic plane as though it were the sole plane of reference, which as already exampled is not true.

Directing for the Solar eclipse on April 17th, 1912, we have:

```
338°41′ RAMC as in last equation
25°08′ R. A. Sun 27°05′♈ at eclipse
3°49′ R. A.  =  M. C. 4°10′♈, near square Mars at event
90°00′
93°49′ O. A. in geocentric lat. 41°34′  =  Asc  22°31′♋.
```

This is near Neptune in 22°36′♋ at the summer solstice. But this is not the main consideration. Rather in this case we must direct the geocentric Ascendant of the place to Neptune (the ship), in 21°04′♋ at the eclipse, **in the plane of Saturn** (the obstruction or iceberg). The equation becomes:

Neptune 21°04′♋ in lat. Saturn 1°58′S = Dec.   19°52′N
Neptune 21°04′♋ in lat. Saturn 1°58′S = R. A. 112°27′

and,

Asc. Diff.	19°52′	tangent	9.557913
Geo. Latitude	41°′34	tangent	9.947827
Declination	18°41′	sine	9.505740

and,

R. A.   112°27′
A. D. —18°41′
O. A.   93°46′.

This is but 3′ less than obtained for the place, as above. Such errors are common when working with Raphael's ephemeris and interpolative tables.

We may direct the Midheaven of the place for the exact time of Uranus' stationary on May 8th, 1912, and obtain 25°29′♈, which is not only near the place of the above Solar eclipse and opposite Mars and square to Neptune at the eclipse on October 10th, 1912, but also the square of Uranus in 25°33′♑ at the eclipse on October 24th, 1911.

This case again warns against expecting striking events at a given place **except the "tangle of world lines" thus couple the place with several eclipses and other inductive celestial configurations.** Just as the heterodyning of several broadcast stations produce chaotic and discordant reception at geographic points where their signal levels are about equal, **so great world events arise at those points where the changes in field strengths produced by eclipses and planetary stationaries are comparatively equally large and the mutual inductions numerous.** The student should here consult Morecroft's text for a clear grasp of mutual induction.

Example 11. The Burning of Alexandria, Egypt.

Pearce, in his **Text-Book of Astrology**, page 327, gives the horary figure of the Solar eclipse, May 17th, 1882, the shadow of which passed over Egypt, and relates it to the burning of Alexandria because, as he states, "Mars was exactly rising" at Cairo at the time of the eclipse. As Mars was actually about six ecliptic degrees below the horizon, it is seen the term "exactly rising" is here very loosely used. Let us see how the precessional equation and annular progressions supplement or rather supersede the horary solution.

> 59°02′ RAMC Alexandria in 1930, Table 1
> —0°37′ Correction to 1882
> (a) 58°25′ R. A. in 1882 = M. C. 0°35′♊
> 53°56′ R. A. of eclipse in 26°15′ ♉
> 112°21′ R. A. = M. C. 19°44′♋.

This is just one hour-angle (15°) from Mars in 4°43′♌ at the time of the eclipse. Of course this is but one of several couplings. It is given as an example of the need of including all of the twenty-four hour-angles, not merely the half of them as texts have taught. This case is also one of many which show electromagnetic couplings should be referred in some cases to the equator. Let us see what is meant by this statement.

Examination of an 1882 ephemeris will show the eclipse occurred in 26°15′ ♉, that Saturn was geocentrically stationary in 26°11′ ♉, and that Mars was opposite in 26 °59′♏ at the November eclipse in that year. As the ecliptic Midheaven was 0°35′♊, as above computed, it is seen to be about 4° east of the longitude of the eclipse and the stationary position of Saturn in their opposition to Mars. Let us see if the conjunction occurred on the equator.

Refer to Fig. 4. RA is the equator and RC is the ecliptic, R being the vernal equinox. Then AB is the Alexandria meridian, cutting the equator at A in R. A. 58°25′ as computed, and intersecting the ecliptic in 0°35′♊ at C. D is 26°11′♉, the longitude of Saturn when stationary, and also within 4′ of the longitude of the eclipse, and DA is the projection of that celestial longitude across the equator. Then to prove that the celestial meridian (DA) of Saturn and the eclipse intersected the terrestrial meridian (AB) of Alexandria on the equator in the right ascension of Alexandria at A, we have the following equation:

Longitude	56°11′ (RD)	cotangent	9.825986	(26°11′ ♉)
Ob. Ec.	23°27′ (ARD)	cosine	9.962562	
R. A.	58°26′ (RA)	cotangent	9.788548	

This is practically the computed R. A. of Alexandria for the ingress of 1882. See (a) in preceding equation.

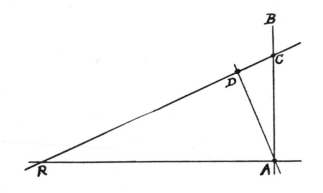

Fig. 4.

Here the question will arise as to under what circumstances the electromagnetic coupling is to be taken in the plane of the **equator.** No complete answer can as yet be given. All that is at present known is that this is the proper equation when the event is one arising out of **acts of reprisal,** as was this one. Why this is so is not difficult to see. The equatorial belt is the one in which the positive and negative polarities of the earth as a spherical magnet **are neutralized or even.** The psy-chological inducement in this plane is therefore one of "**getting even.**" In connection with example 6 it would be easy to show that the Solar eclipses in 2°08′ ♒ and 6°44′ ♌ were in almost exact **equatorial** opposition. This should be kept in mind in considering the origin of that event.

Example 12. The New York subway accident, August 24th, 1928.

By inspection of Table I we see that in 1928 the M. C. of New York was in 12°39′ ♒, and Ascendant in 6°35′ ♊. The Lunar eclipse on June 3rd, 1928, occurred in 12°38′ ♐, near Saturn, trine to Mars and exactly sextile to the New York Mid-heaven. On the day of the event Saturn excited this coupling by transiting 12°34′ ♐, over the place of the Moon at its eclipse. Uranus at the time of this eclipse was in 6°47′ ♈*, sextile to the Ascendant, and it had returned to 6°42′ ♈ on the day of event.

Now a few directions.

It is shown in Fig. 3 in **The Stars, How and Where They Influence,** that at the June eclipse Mars was in 13°14′ ♈ in R. A. or mundo conjunction with star No. 175 in the field plane of Saturn. This star circling in the **latitude** of New York. Let us see how the Solar eclipse of May 19th, 1928, brought out this field coupling in the **longitude** of New York. Solution:

315°09′ RAMC New York for 1928, Table J reduction.
56°19′ R. A. east limb of Sun (28°33′ ♉) at eclipse in
   28°17′ ♉.

371°28′
360°00′ Reject circle

11°28′ R. A. progressed M. C.

This is precisely the R. A. of the star and of Mars' longitude in the plane of Saturn, as shown in Fig. 3 of the companion text mentioned above.

Directing the New York 3rd electric axis or "house"—ruler of transportation lines—we have

---

* Conjunction with star No. 85. See Fig. 4 in **The Stars, How and Where They Influence.**

315°09′ RAMC New York at ingress, as above
153°30′ R. A. Sun 1°29′♍ at the accident
_____
108°39′ RAMC (After rejecting circle)
150°00′ For 3rd axis
_____
258°39′ O. A. 3rd (geo. pole 16°13′) = 3rd angle 13°11′ ♐

This is a trine to Mars in 13°14′♈ at the June eclipse, and a close conjunction with the place of the eclipsed Moon in 12°38′ ♐ .

To show how the post-event Solar eclipse on November 12th, 1928, coupled the New York Ascendant with Mars, the June eclipse, and star No. 175, we have:

315°09′ RAMC as in foregoing equations
227°19′ R. A. Sun at eclipse in 19°46′♍
_____
182°28′ RAMC progressed (Add and reject circle)
 90°00′
_____
272°28′ O. A. in latitude 40°44′ = Asc. 13°14′ ♐ .

This is the exact trine of Mars in 13°14′♈ and near the place of the eclipsed Moon in 12°38′ ♐ . These equations show that even a trine of Mars to an eclipse may signify accidents at points longitudinally and latitudinally coupled therewith when the exciting transit is adverse, as Saturn conjunction eclipse in this case. Also Mars transiting the New York Ascendant in opposition to Saturn.

Example 13. The Elba, Alabama, flood, March 15-16, 1929.

Scaled from a map the location is 86°05′W and 31°27′N.

29°09′ RAMC Greenwich in 1929, Table I
360°00′ Add circle to subtract longitude
_____
389°09′
—86°05′ Longitude of Elba, West.
_____
303°04′ RAMC Elba in 1929
 90°00′ For horizon
_____
393°04′
360°00′ Reject circle
_____
 33°04′ O. A. in geocentric lat. 31°17′ = Asc. 16°01′ ♉

The Solar eclipse on May 9th, 1929, occurs in 18°07′ ♉. The beginner will be inclined to tolerate this wide orb, even though it represents an apparent error of well over one hundred miles. The true solution, however, is found in the fact that if we direct the Elba Midheaven to the date of the flood's crest we find the place of Mars at this eclipse was passing the Nadir. This indicated the destruction to property. Therefore we should look for the locality Ascendant at the ingress to couple with the eclipse **in the field plane of Mars,** which was in 1°44′N. Hence we have:

Long. eclipse in 18°07′ ♉ in lat. 1°44′N = Dec. 18°53′N
Long. eclipse in 18°07′ ♉ in lat. 1°44′N = R. A. 45°08′

and,

Declination	18°53′	tangent	9.534504
Geo. latitude	31°17′	tangent	9.783626
Asc. Diff.	12°01′	sine	9.318130

and,

R. A.	45°08′
A. D.	—12°01′
O. A.	33°07′

This agrees with the computed O. A. of Elba's Ascendant within three miles—the limit of interpolative accuracy.

If we direct the Elba Midheaven for this eclipse we find it sextile to the eclipse and trine to Mars' longitude at the autumn, 1929, eclipse. This is important only because Mars at the latter eclipse is opposite the spring eclipse on the Elba Ascendant. But the most significant direction is that of the November eclipse, as follows:

303°04′	RAMC Elba 1929, as preceding equation
216°12′	R. A. Sun 8°35′♏ at eclipse Nov. 1st, 1929.
519°16′	
360°00	Reject circle
159°16′	RAMC progressed.
—90°00′	
69°16′	O. D. (oblique descension) of western horizon.

At the time of the eclipse on May 9th, Neptune was **stationary** in 28°35′♌, in latitude 0°36′N. And to prove the above O. D. is that required to bring the Descendant square to Neptune in Neptune's field, we have the following equations:

Square of Neptune, 28°35′ ♉, in lat. 0°36′N = Dec. 20°26′N
Square of Neptune, 28°35′ ♉, in lat. 0°36′N = R. A. 56°11′

and,

Declination	20°26′	tangent	9.571195
Geo. lat.	31°17′	tangent	9.783626
Asc. Diff.	13°05′	sine	9.354821
R. A.	56°11′		
O. D.	69°16′ as above		

The novice may wonder why in this case the Descendant is brought to the square of Neptune instead of directing the Ascendant to the opposite square. Simply because the rain and flood (Neptune) descended (Descendant) upon the town. Some may even think the Ascendant and Decendant arcs to the square of Neptune are equal, and so they would be if taken on the ecliptic, but not so when taken in the latitude or radial field of a planet. To make the Ascendant arc equal would require taking 0°36′ **south** latitude, but as the planet is **north** such a practice would be unwarranted, **though the equivalent of such an error is found scattered all through the standard astrological texts.** Opposite angles do not direct to planets **in latitude** at the **same time,** as most students and practicing astrologers seem to think. This could be easily shown by mathematics and a diagram, but such is not within the scope of this text. Those mathematically inclined can easily prove this point for themselves.

It may be helpful to observe that on the days of the flood Mercury transited opposite Neptune and over the longitude of star No. 5845*, which circles latitudinally nadir to Elba. What

---

*   Boss Catalogue.

this means will be clear to those studying the text on the stars.

In Table I it is easy to see the Solar eclipse on May 9th, 1929, in 18°07' ♉, centers on the Ascendant along a line from Wisconsin to Florida. Also across Panama, Columbia, Bolivia and Argentina. Note the Bolivia-Paraguay boundary dispute and the earthquake May 30th, 1929, in the Mendoza district of Argentina. A little farther west lies the line of Ascendant 105° (7-hour angle) from Neptune, 75° from Mars, and sesqui-quadrate to Saturn, as they are placed at the time of eclipse. The precessional horizon thus computed for its intersections with the several different planes of the planetary electromagnetic fields, determines the storm and flood areas along that general eclipse belt. If the electromagnetic couplings were effectual only in the ecliptic plane there would be but one narrow and oblique path involved. The fact that simultaneous storm or flood centers dot an **irregular path** should convince the student he ought not ignore the latitudes of the planets because it simplifies the calculations to do so. Very little electrical and astronomical investigation will convince him how crude is the prevailing astrological practice of computing mutual induction only in the ecliptic plane.

Example 14. The Florida bank failures, July, 1929.

Relative to the closing of the Citizens Bank and Trust Company of Tampa, and of its neighboring branches, on July 17th, 1929, the computer will find the precessional Ascendant of Tampa and vicinity **was exactly conjunction with the May eclipse taken in the field plane of Jupiter and Uranus at that eclipse.** Jupiter signifies financial institutions and Uranus denotes "runs" or panics. This coupling was excited by Uranus **stationary** in middle July, and on July 17th the Sun transited the 105° axis of Uranus' place at the eclipse.

Directing Tampa for this eclipse brings its 2nd angle to 27°55'♋, which is precisely the longitude of Mars at the eclipse. The 2nd angle refers to finance and Mars to "breaks" or losses. Directing Tampa for July 17th shows the square of Mars to Jupiter on that date falls on the annular horizon and zenith of that city on July 17th to 19th.

At the eclipse on Nov. 1st, 1929, Tampa's Ascendant is $3°\,\ddagger$, square to Neptune in $3°15'\mathrm{m}$ at that eclipse. And to show that Neptune was then on the precessional 5th (banks) angle of Tampa, taken in the plane of Uranus (the "run") at the May eclipse, we have the following equations:

> 306°42′ RAMC Tampa in 1929, Table I reduction
> —150°00′ 5th angle converse from M. C.
> 156°42′ O. D. (oblique descension) 5th angle

and,

>   R. A 154°56′ =Neptune $3°15'\mathrm{m}$ in lat. Uranus 0°41′S
> 1/3 A. D.   1°44′ =Neptune $3°15'\mathrm{m}$ in lat. Uranus 0°41′S
>   O. D. 156°40′, as above, within two miles

This examples a coupling at one eclipse taken in the field of a planet at another eclipse within the year.

All calculations for this event are made for **geographic** latitude because the event is one depending on organic or psy-chologic agencies and so involves the spheroidal equations rather than the spherical (geocentric) equation of inorganic crystals such as the earth must be viewed when computing its oscillation axes in relation to earthquakes. Review Chapter II on this point. Those studying the companion text will find it instructive to compute the couplings of the eclipse figures with stars whose radial fields cut central Florida.

Example 15. The Mexican Revolution, 1929.

The first thing to note is that the May eclipse in $18°07'\,\vartheta$ occurs in oppositon to the longitude of Mars in $17°55'\mathrm{m}$ at the November eclipse. Then turning to Table I it will be seen this cross configuration closely aspects the meridian of Mexico City in $18°30'\,\text{vs}$ in the current year. Mars at the spring eclipse is in 27°55′♋, in square to the Ascendant of such Mexican points as the capital, Tampico, etc.

The student should note that Uranus was on the Mexico Midheaven and in opposition to Neptune on its Nadir when Mexico was in a state of chaos (Neptune) through the series of counter-revolutions (Uranus) preceding the World War. In 1931 Saturn will transit the meridian of Mexico City, in square to Uranus on its western Ascendant.

From the nature of all these examples the casual reader may erroneously infer that eclipses are to be viewed, if not with the ancient fears aroused by them, at least as rather bad form on the part of our celestial neighbors. But these events are chosen for examples solely because they are more widely known and better remembered than is much of the good that could be cited. For instance, Jupiter dominates the May eclipse and configures the site of Boulder Dam†, where Congress has voted to spend millions for power and irrigation development and for flood control. The good Samaritan (Jupiter) and his charming lady (Venus) have their geographic places of "honorable mention" at eclipses just as much as tempestuous Mars, surly or severe Saturn, revolutionary Uranus, and the rest of the soul's (Sun's) "plan it" (planet) cabinet.

It is true, however, that a **Solar** eclipse when expressing through an afflicting planet means placing good or bad common sense (the Moon) **before** wisdom (the Sun) and interjecting a "dark horse" into the "brightest" scheme, and that human nature looks into things as into a mirror (Moon) placed

---

† Directing the eclipse converse, as the vote preceded it, brings Jupiter's longitude at the eclipse to the Nadir at the proposed dam sites. The Nadir refers to building, land and land reclaimation, and Jupiter is the "greater benefic." The precessional Ascendant of Boulder Canyon is at this epoch about 7° Aries. Uranus transiting that point refers to the power and engineering development of the project. Uranus on the Ascendant of the boundary line between California and Arizona also refers to the disagreement between these states over the division of water and power. Those interested in the Mississippi flood control question and the Muscle Shoals issue may easily see from Table I when Uranus will reach the Ascendants of those regions.

in a dark room, rather than sees through things as sunlight through unsilvered glass.

It is equally true that a **Lunar** eclipse is a condition under which the "current" of affairs then set up **reflect** (Moon) little or none of the wisdom (Sun) which ordinarily by a full Moon or a full knowledge lights the dark hours of man's pilgrimage; this because of the intervention of a crass material' ism (the earth) between the eye of Wisdom (Sun) and the eye of Knowledge (Moon).

The stationary angles of the planets simply define the re' versal of "current trends." Mutual conjunctions unify or com' bine forces. Oppositions define the conflicts of opposing fac' tions and rival interests and the struggle to maintain "the balance of power" between them. Squares denote crossroads, intervention or interference, a squaring up of business or ac' counts or long delayed issues, or the interjection of still other delays and cross currents. But they also mean, as electrical law defines, a neutralization of mutual induction. Trine angles are found to denote the maximum constructive striving—the rewards of persistent trying, trial or experiment. A sextile is a good half'try. A semisquare defines those issues which are but half'way "on the square." And so on.

It is thus precisely because all these inductive couplings are forever changing, owing to the constant movements of the charged celestial bodies, that it takes all kinds of people and all kinds of events to make a world; that is, to make up a whorl or precessional cycle at the end of which man discovers the persistence of a lot of vanity and a mere trace of perma' nent evolution.

To avoid complexity nothing has been said in these ex' amples about the **ecliptic** arc of direction given in formula (5), Chapter IV. These arcs of "inducement" will be briefly ex' ampled in the next chapter. But in a comprehensive study of such world events as war, or those which arise through the mediumship of man and are not so easily directly saddled upon "Nature" as are storms and earthquakes, it is necessary to include directions by the ecliptic arcs as well as those by the right ascensional arcs such as have been exampled.

Space will not admit of citing a series of examples, but one will here be given to point the way.

It was shown in example 6 the blowing up of the Maine was indicated in the Washington equation by advancing its meridian to Uranus by the **R. A.** arc of the Lunar eclipse on January 7th, 1898. As a "current event" that equation defines the incident. But as an "inducement" (ecliptic arc) to the hard feelings (Saturn) towards Spain, which followed this incident, we have, among the **several** couplings, the following ecliptic equation:

309°43' Long. Washington M. C. 9°43'♒, Table I
—0°24' Correction to 1898 (32 yrs. × .'76)
309°19' Long. Washington 1898
302°08' Long. Sun 2°08'♒ at Solar eclipse Jan. 22nd, 1898
611°27'
600°00' Subtract 20 signs (circle plus 8 signs)
 11°27' ♐ Washington Midheaven by ecliptic arc

Inspection of an 1898 ephemeris will show **that Saturn passed the exact conjunction of this point on April 22nd, 1898, when the war began.** The arc is taken for a **Solar** eclipse as the declaration of war was an official (Sun) act. The **R. A.** arc cited in example 6 is taken for the **Lunar** eclipse because the sinking of the Maine was a lunar act of "one of the people," or a crazy plot of a few thereof, and due to a **reprisal** notion set up in them by the **equatorial** oppositon of the two eclipses, as mentioned in example 11.

CHAPTER VI

APPLICATION TO NATIVITIES

From the individual point of view what part does location play in success or failure, in health or sickness, in content or discontent, in friendship or family relations and in all the vital concerns of life?

After years of study and service in relation to the problem of aiding individuals to find their places in the world, geographically as much as vocationally, it is the author's opinion that location is all the way from twenty-five to seventy-five per cent, or more, of the secret of results. In this view the author is not alone*.

The importance of location is stated broadly because undoubtedly location plays a larger part in some lives than in others, or rather some are so qualified and destined for major success that they will make a more or less successful showing anywhere, while others have such indifferent abilities that no location will make them really successful. Broadly speaking, genius is genius anywhere; an idiot remains an idiot in any retreat. But these anomalies are the exception, not the rule. The average person is susceptible to the forces of improvement and detriment.

What is meant by a suitable location is one wherein the best promise of the nativity is the most intensified and the detrimental qualities are the most minimized†. If the individual's planets — his scheme of "plan its" — are all favorably

---

* See Raphael's **Key to Astrology**, pages 82-83.

† Electrically speaking "close coupled" and "loose coupled."

placed and rayed, which is rarely indeed the case, it is still possible to amplify their effects in one location and suppress them in another and so enlarge or limit his success. If the planetary couplings are mostly adverse it is still generally possible, except of the hopelessly foolish, idiotic or criminal, to change the relative intensity of different qualities in such a manner as to modify the life tendencies. In the average horoscope, however, there is found such an admixture of good and detrimental qualities that the problem becomes one of calculating a place where the good is brought out and the ill suppressed.

How is this possible? Simply by intelligently taking advantage of electromagnetic laws as electrical engineering has revealed them and accepting without further delay, excusable only by virtue of human vanity, the shortly unescapable fact **that these laws apply to the entire universe and constitute the Invisible Power which man in all ages has instinctively designated as God.**

There is no reason for man to become more atheistic, less reverential of the gifts with which he is intrusted, simply because he may come to view either God's love or His alleged wrath in such other terms—gravitation or magnetism, for instance—as scientific separatists and specialists have seen fit for engineering purposes to label it. To those with a larger sense of unity, and blessed with "the eye that sees singly," a rose by any other name is none the less sweet. With respect to the universal law of attraction which binds up the cosmos, it is not the label we give it that matters. It is the good or bad **engineering** of it that decides the results. That is man's supreme business. Modern psychologists recognize this by stressing behaviorism as the goal of all knowledge.

To speak, then, in terms none the less "religious" because using the language of science, it may be said that **the life of the individual is in all respects the sum of the electromagnetic mo-**

tivations of all the inductive couplings of all the charged bodies in the universe as their fields interact at the moment of his birth, and as superimposed upon the same set of factors as they exist at the time of conception. But when we read a nativity we read the life at the birthplace. And this is subject to modification for all other localities. Let us see why this is so.

It is an electrical law that if we change the relative positions of two or more electrically charged bodies—such as are stars, suns, planets, earth, and man upon the earth—either as to their angular relations or distances, **we change their phase angles and the degree of mutual induction between them at any given point in their fields.**

It thus comes about that as the planets and earth change their mutual relations in space in the days following birth their electromagnetic couplings are so changed and their new inductive phases so impressed upon the formative life of the child* as to motive its life accordingly from year to year. It is thus the **progressed** horoscope defines the crises in life, and thus that individuals change their ways (or "plan its") for better or worse from time to time; each by a pattern unique, since not in millions of years can the same **complete** set of electromagnetic couplings repeat†. Like couplings are found only in some cases of twins. And only then insofar as the **birth minutes** coincide.

Over the relative positions and movements of the stars, planets and earth, man has no control, no choice. They may be likened to a number of broadcast stations authorized by a Fed-

---

* Whether by changes in the blood plasm or in the brain cells is as yet unknown. This will be determined in the future by experiments with high frequency oscillators relative to the psychological and physiological reactions of individuals and groups subjected to such waves at close range. The effect of three to five meter waves on body temperature and upon the sodium chloride of the blood has already been noted by several experimenters. Between waves of such length and those of the light spectrum there remains an unexplored realm of miracles closely bound up with unfathomed dangers.

† The skeptic is here invited to compute for himself the least common multiple of the orbital periods of the Moon and planets—not to mention the proper motion of the stars.

eral Commission to operate here and there for the good of the populace, but with little regard for the kind of reception received by any particular individual happily or adversely placed with respect to the heterodyning of their programs.

But as in radio, so in human life. If the reception is poor or chaotic, oversensitive in one direction and unselective in another, and he cannot adapt his particular set (himself) to receive anything good from the heterodyning stations (planets, stars), **he is at least free to remove his set (himself) elsewhere where reception is better for his particular type of receiver (his pyschologic type)**.

No matter what the admixture of planetary waves at his birthplace, if he moves elsewhere he, as a charged body, **inevitably changes the inductive coupling of his personal electromagnetic field with respect to those of all the planets and stars.** As a result different qualities and "inducements" will arise, latent characteristics will be intensified and old ones modified or neutralized. He will "attract" and "repulse" different types of associates, just as a magnet reverses its poles when the direction of the inducing current is reversed, or the coil is reversed. And his character, health and circumstances will undergo from moderate to startling changes according to the degree of change in the inductive couplings. He may, as is often the case, so change his life as to better his health and deplete his purse, or from meanness evolve nobility only to put himself in the way of a fatal accident. For it generally "happens" that no one place can be recommended in every respect. We choose and pay. But that is no reason we should forever choose **blindly** in matters of more human moment than those which today engage the best engineering skill.

All this does not mean the greatest change in the human equation will always be brought about by going to the antipodes. Far from it. In one case a few degrees of longitude and latitude will perfect a desirable electromagnetic coupling which in another case might require a transfer to another country or continent. In practice the aim must as often be to perfect the aspect (eliminate the orb) existing as to change it into a coupling defined by a different electrical axis (aspect).

It may here be objected by fatalistic astrologers and lay-men that if the individual is so constituted at birth as to respond or tune to, let us say, the "plan it" or psychologic frequency of Mars*, his removal from the town of A to the town of B will in no way change his "vibration" to put him in tune with the wavelength of Jupiter, and that therefore he must continue to dance to his Mars program or else not dance at all. Such reasoning is both true and false. In the first place, if his Mars is favorably qualified the aim would not be to induce him to locate with consideration to a Jupiter coupling, but rather to so locate him as to bring in his Mars station (in life) more strongly by closer coupling of its field and his field. Further, as the electrophysicist is well aware, the too prevalent supposition that a man or a radio can respond only to the wavelength to which they are tuned, is but **relatively** true. For just as the resistance of a tuned circuit to a distance-weakened wave of the same frequency may be greater than the resistance of an untuned circuit to the wave of a local transmitter, so the individual tuned to Mars, if removed far from the direct radial field of Mars and close coupled with that of Jupiter may, despite his untuned relation to the latter, respond only to the program of Jupiter; though **under an equal degree of coupling** he would of course respond only to Mars.

In other words, Man's sensitivity and selectivity depend, as do those of a radio, not entirely upon the tuning, but upon the **relative wave strengths at a given place.** If the signal

---

* The natural and harmonic frequencies of a planet depend on its elements, density, mass and diameter, precisely as does that of a small quartz crystal used as frequency controls in radio transmitters.

level is strong enough to overcome the resistance of the circuit, the radio or the man will respond whether or no they are in tune with the signal, though if untuned the man will not respond to the same degree he may "in time" when his progressed horoscope brings him under another planet or wavelength. Therefore while it is true that tuning lowers the resistance to a program, there is another alternative—that of raising the signal level by closer location with a desired station, "plan it" or planet. By this is not meant that change of location significantly changes the actual radial distance between the man and a planet, since even the antipodes or the earth's diameter is negligible relative to the distances of the planets from the earth, but change of location accomplishes what comes to the same thing; namely,**increased or decreased mutual induction through phase changes due to different angular relations between the planet's and the man's electric and magnetic fields.**

The complete exposition of these astrological truths which harmonize electrical law and observations would fill several large volumes. And because the principles involved necessitate the projection of the entire personal horoscope in both latitude and longitude*, it must not be supposed their application to the world horoscope, as in this volume and in that on the fixed stars, by any means exhausts the subject.

Though the greater changes in **personal** psychology which relocation tends to bring about, depend upon the projection of the **horary** nativity, the rules for which are outside the scope of this work, nevertheless in a study of the individual's relation to the **community** life of his town, or to the **national life,** it is helpful to set up the precessional cusps†of the place for his birth year and to plot therein the planet's places at his birth. This, however, is as far from the **main** consideration as

* A condensed text on this will be undertaken if the demand justifies it.
† As in Table I.

it would be to attempt to read all world events from the transits through the precessional cusps, against which the student is warned in Chaper IV.

It should be plain that just as the precessional angles or electrical axes of a locality may be and must be directed on the solar arc to the dates of eclipses, planetary stationaries and other inductive phenomena and to the times of world events, so, too, they may be and must be directed to **the birthday of the individual under study, and in exactly the same manner— by solar arcs—as though his birth was an eclipse or any other elective time, as for him such it is.**

It is a good plan to designate such a figure, compounded of the native's planetary positions and the locality angles for his birthday, as **"The Birthday Locality."** The individual's birth hour does not enter into the calculation at all except as it moderately affects the longitudes of the planets in the figure and the longitude of the Sun from which the solar arc is derived for progressing the cusps for the equinox to the date of birth. Thus the **"Birthday Locality"** (hereinafter abbreviated to BL) angles may be computed within one degree of error† for any person for any place even when the birth hour is entirely unknown, and thus much useful information can often be given the individual who otherwise cannot be served at all because of the many cases in which the birth minute is unknown for setting up or directing a horary nativity after the manner of standard texts. This the examples will clarify.

It will be plain that since the positions of the electrical axes in a BL figure depend upon the solar longitude, they will differ, for any given place, for all individuals born on different days of the year, slightly so for those of the same day in either different precessional epochs or at different hours. Even if the solar longitude is the same in two cases and so gives the

---

† The approximate amount the Solar or earth's couplings change daily.

same or nearly the same Midheavens and Ascendants at a given place, if the year is different all the other planets and the Moon will be differently placed in the figure and the connections with the community or national life will be, in most cases, quite different. It is as rare to encounter duplicate BL figures as it is to find any two **horary** nativities alike in more than a few respects at most. All this will be readily clear from the examples to follow and from a little personal practice; even if to some the procedure should appear on first reading as either tedious or involved.

It must be constantly kept in mind that this work is confined to world equations in **longitude.** These figures relate to **latitude** only insofar as latitude tilts the oblique sphere and so shifts the oblique angles. **The principal consideration in the latitudinal equation is the fixed stars,** and their couplings with places and planets are explained and exampled in the author's companion work thereon. These texts go together as equal halves of a complete geographic equation.

The question will now arise as to whether the BL figures can be or should be **directed** on the native's solar arcs. **They assuredly can be and must be. That is a dominant consideration,** as the examples will show. The progressive sweep of ones planets over the BL angles, or vice versa, will be found to explain many events of combined personal and community import which would not be easily deduced from the horary nativity and its directions alone.

Whether the calculation of the BL Midheaven and Ascendant, and their directions to events in the life, is to be taken by the **right ascension** of the solar arc as applied to the **right ascension** of the precessional (equinoctial) Midheaven of the place as calculated in Table I, and known as the Placidian arc, as exampled by equation (4) Chapter IV, or is to be taken by the **ecliptic** solar arc and applied to the **ecliptic longitude** of the precessional Midheaven as exampled by equation (5) Chapter IV†, depends on whether the purpose is a study of the individual's relation to the "current events" (R. A. arc or plane) of the community or national life, or a study of the "inducements" (ecliptic arcs or plane) the place offers him, or the measure of his influence thereon.

At this point the beginner must study very carefully the distinction made in Chapter IV. Perhaps to the average astrological student, unfamiliar with electrodynamics, no exposition of electrical laws will clear his mind on this important consideration unless he applies both arcs of direction in every case and learns by actual observation the kinds of events they respectively bring about. The proof of any theory is the untiring test thereof. Here again the last word probably can never be written. At least where the lifetime of one generation is required to disclose the few basic principles, another generation or two is required to sift the evidence and refine their applications.

In applying solar arcs, both right ascensional and ecliptic, to both horary nativities and BL figures, there is one technicality which must be considered that does not apply to directing eclipses for world events after the manner of Chapters IV and V. It is this: **In directing nativities and BL figures, a sidereal day is to be taken for a year of life in lieu of the common practice of using the solar day.** A complete explanation of the reasons for this, and a set of tables for applying the correctives to the regular astrological ephemeris, is the work of another text.

For all purposes of the present work it suffices to say the true sidereal solar arc can be found by computing the Placidian arcs in R. A. and ecliptic and **reducing them by one minute of arc for each six years of life.** More exactly the correction amounts to 5′ at the age of 31 and 10′ at 62, and like

---

† For directing BL figures see Case 2 for methods of computing arcs.

proportions for other ages. Expressed in time the correction becomes 3'56" per year, amounting to an hour in a trifle over every 15 years of life. It is here taken for granted the stu' dent is familiar with the calculation of Placidian arcs, as their R. A. equation is fully explained in several standard texts†. However, the calculation of the arcs will be found in connec' tion with **Case 2** of the examples which follow. Refer to the foregoing when studying them.

The reader is here advised that he cannot expect to obtain any satisfactory results with this text if he insists on directing the angles by either the astronomically and electrically ground' less Ptolemaic arc, or by any of the equally erroneous methods advanced in many astrological texts. Such as, for instance, directing the Midheaven an even degree a year in all cases, or directing it by sidereal time without taking into consideration what is astronomically known as "the equation of time." A separate text is required to reveal all the errors into which mathematical astrologers have fallen in the past because of the deficiency of their astronomical training and their disregard for the electrical laws which alone can advance astrology to its rightful place among the exact sciences and explain how and why planets and stars are the source of all our inducements, righteousness, obliquities and motivations, and how God or the Invisible Power rules the world and all mankind.

Let us now turn to a few illuminating examples of the purpose of this chapter to show how and **where** this Power sets the stage for the individual, and why The Play is different as the stage is moved.

Case 1. As a first example let us take King Edward VII, born November 9th, 1841, at 10.48 A. M. official time*,

† Zadkiel's **Grammar of Astrology**, Pearce's **Textbook of Astrology**, Leo's **The Progressed Horoscope.**

* The true time of birth rectifies to 10.32 A. M. by the horary nativity, but this makes no measurable difference whatever in the progression of the locality figure.

London.   The horary nativity is given on page 195 of Pearce's
text.   The accompanying figure shows the planets' positions
in the BL piezoelectric angles (astrologically termed "house
divisions") of London for his epoch and date.   The calculation is as follows:

> 29°03′ R. A. London in 1930, Table 1
> −·1°09′ Correction to 1841 (89 yrs. × 46″.10)
> ――――
> 27°54′ R. A. London 1841 = M. C. 0°00′ ♉ †
> 224°26′ R. A. Sun 16°54′♏, as in the figure
> (a) 252°20′ R. A. of BL = M. C. 13°43′♏
>   90°00′
> ――――
> 342°20′ O. A. in latitude 51°19′ = 21°07′ ♒ Asc.

The Ascendant is here calculated for geocentric latitude,
but for some purposes the geographic equation should be used,
as previously explained.   It will be seen that the planets were
well elevated in the BL figure and that the Ascendant was sextile to Jupiter in the Midheaven.   The foregoing calculation is
for the **right ascensional** (Placidian) arc.   The corresponding
ecliptic equation becomes:

> 30°00′ Long. London M. C. in 1841 (0°00′ ♉)
> 226°′54 Long. Sun in 16°54′♏
> (b) 256°54′ BL M. C. = 16°54′ ♐ ,

semi-sextile to the Sun in 16°54′♏.   This is obtained by subtracting eight signs (240°); no R. A. arc entering into this
measure at all.

As in the BL figure Venus and the Sun were in the VIIIth
house (heritage), we would expect these to be directed to at
the death of the Queen mother and his accession to the throne.
Let us see if this is so, directing respectively by both R. A. and
ecliptic solar sidereal arcs from these foregoing Midheavens.

> 252°20′ R. A. of BL M. C. as per (a)
> 63°51′ Solar sidereal arc in R. A. for his age at event*
> ――――
> 316°11′ Prog. RAMC = 13°43′♒, sextile BL M. C. and con-
>   junction with Neptune in the latitude of Venus

―――――――――――――――――――――――――――――――――
† Trine to his rising Saturn.

And for the Ascendant, we have:

> 361°11' Progressed RAMC
> 90°00'
> _____
> 406°11' (a)
> 360°00' Reject circle when (a) exceeds it
> _____
> 46°11' O. A. in latitude 51°19' = Asc. 19°14'♊,

This is seen to be the exact trine of Venus in 19°14'♎ on the VIIIth angle.

And,

> 256°54' Long. of BL M. C. as per (b).
> 59°57' Solar sidereal arc on ecliptic for event*.
> _____
> 316°51'
> 300°00' Subtract ten signs.
> _____
> 16°51'♒

This is the square of the Sun in 16°54'♏ in the BL VIIIth. If the Ascendant is computed for this equation it will be found to be a little past the oppositon of Jupiter in the BL zenith.

As in his horary nativity the Sun was in the zenith and square to Neptune, it is consistent to find the BL Midheavens respectively conjunction with Neptune and square to the Sun at this event. In the first equation the zenith square to Neptune is taken in the plane of Venus because the Ascendant was trine thereto and because Venus held the VIIIth angle. In the second equation the arc is taken on the ecliptic as the Sun has no latitude. The direction of the Ascendant is taken for the geocentric latitude of London because the mother's death was neither an event to his person nor one into which his volition entered†.

Next let us direct the BL figure for the time of death, May 6th, 1910, as follows:

---

* These arcs are obtained by the methods explained in next case, as are also all directional arcs used in this Chapter.

† See Chapter II, explanation of columns 6 and 8 of Table I.

252'20° R. A. as per (a)
73°52′ Solar sidereal arc in R. A. at event*
326°12′ Prog. RAMC = 23°53′♒.

This is close trine with George Vth's progressed Saturn in 23°56′♎, to whom the great responsibilities of the throne descended at this event.

Adding to this RAMC 90° for the Ascendant and rejecting the circle, we obtain O. A. 56°12′, and this under the **geographic** latitude of London gives the progressed Ascendant 29°21′♊, which is the square of the Moon in 29°24′♍ in the **rectified** horary nativity. The direction is taken in geographic latitude as the event is personal.

Directing on the ecliptic arc we have:

256°54′   M. C. as per (b)
69°23′   Solar sidereal arc in longitude at event*
326°17′
300°00′   Subtract ten signs
26°17′♒

And to direct the Ascendant for this equation we have:

328°31′   R. A. of 26°17′♒
90°00′
418°31′
360°00′ Reject circle
58°31′ O. A. progressed Asc.

To show that this is nearly the exact O. A. required to bring the Asc. opposite Saturn in its own plane (latitude), we have the following ascensional difference equation:

Dec. Saturn	22°44′	tangent	9.622207
Lat. London	51°30′	tangent	0.099395
A. D.	31°47′	sine	9.721602

and,

90°12′ R. A. opposition Saturn 0°11′♑ in Lat. 0°43′N.
—31°47′ A. D.
58°25′ O. A.

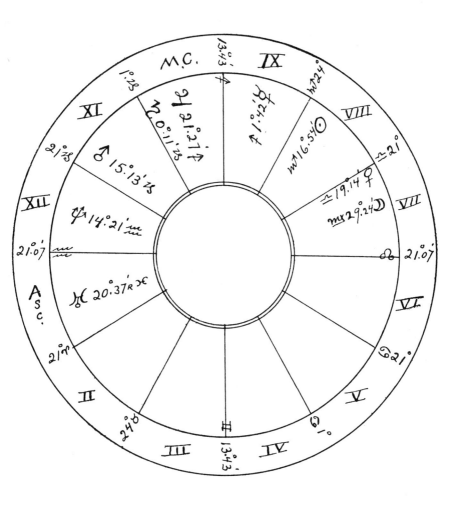

EDWARD VII

Birthday Locality at London

This is 6′ less than the above O. A. of Ascendant, but still bringing the coupling within the limits of London.

Therefore at His Majesty's death the London Ascendant by R. A. and ecliptic arcs was respectively square to the Moon and opposite Saturn. This would be expected from the fact that in his horary nativity Saturn was rising in square to the Moon. In fact one of the exact arcs in the horary horoscope for that time is, when correctly equated, Moon opposite Saturn by primary direction.

If we direct the BL figure on the R. A. arc for the time of his marriage we obtain M. C. 4°11′♑, which is just a five-hour angle (75°) from Venus. This is one of the additional aspects mentioned earlier in this work and in many magazine articles by the author. It should in all cases be used in lieu of the quintile (72°).

Directing in the same manner we find the BL M. C. passed his progressed Saturn during the year he lost his father. In the year bringing the Boer War the M. C. passed the semi-sextile of Mars (war) and had arrived at the conjunction of his progressed Neptune (sedition) at the opening of the rebellion. No astrologer familiar with the nature of planets and angles can say any of these directions are not strictly consistent with what horary nativities and standard astrological texts have taught him. Moreover, the superior elevation of Jupiter, Mercury and Sun was a clear indication of his popularity and peaceful reign, the Boer War terminating but a little over a year after his accession.

Case 2. His Majesty George V, born June 3rd, 1865, 1:18 A. M., London. Sun 12°26′♊.

```
  29°03′  R. A. London in 1930, Table I
 —0°50′   Correction to 1865 (65 yrs. × 46″.10)
 ────────
  28°13   R. A. London 1865  =  M. C. 0°20′♉
  70°58′  R. A. Sun in 12°26′♊ at birth
```
(a)   99°11′ R. A. of BL = M. C. 8°24′♋. Asc. is 6″30′♎.

And,

> 30°20′ Long. London M. C. 1865, (0°20′ ♉)
> 72°26′ Long. Sun 12°26′♊
> (b) 102°46′ Long. BL M. C. = 12°46′♋. Asc. 9°48′♎.

The accompanying figure shows the planets' longitudes plotted in the BL angles as computed by (a), the planets being in the same general elevation in the ecliptic equation (b). We notice at once that this is not in some respects as favored a figure for His Majesty or for England as was that of his father. Here Jupiter is low in the figure rather than high. Uranus, the ruler of strikes, labor and industrial upheavals, revolutions† and a divided government, was elevated near the zenith, and following it into elevation was Mars, the lord of war. Saturn was rising in the Ascendant, showing the ascendency of the Labor (Saturn) Party during his reign*; also the personal sacrifices and those of the people in the long dark days of the Great War. Jupiter in the IIIrd house (elder brother) and sextile to the rising Saturn denoted his elevation to the throne and its heavy responsibilities through the death of the heir apparent. Therefore we should expect to find the BL figure direct to Jupiter and Saturn when he acceded upon the death of Edward VII in 1910. Testing this we find:

---

† As to revolutions, referring to the Russian and German revolts attending the Great War, and to the coming complete, though possibly more peaceful, breakup of the British Empire about the close of George V's reign—as Uranus held the nadir of his nativity and is near the zenith of his BL figure, and because of the slow transit of Uranus over the Midheaven of the British Isles from 1932 (West Ireland) to 1936 (East England), centering over London in 1934 and 1935. This is followed by Uranus to the 11th angle of London in 1943-44, as in 1776, when, if not before, Britain may expect complete severance from her most important colonies. Great political and economic upheavals in England and Europe will attend the transit of Uranus over their zeniths as given in Table I.

* This was written in February, 1929, before Labor's second election on May 31st.

```
 99°11'  R. A. of BL M. C. as per (a)
 46°10'  Solar sidereal arc in R. A. at accession
─────────
145°21'  Prog. RAMC  =  23°00'♌
180°00'
─────────
325°21'  Prog. R. A. of IVth house (the father).
```

This is the right ascension of 23°56'♒, the trine of progressed Saturn 23°56'♎ at event, in the latitude of natal Saturn
and Neptune in 2°39'N; as 23°56'♒ in 2°39'N gives R. A.
325°22'.

And,

```
102°46'   Long. BL M. C. as per ( b)
 42°45'   Solar sidereal arc in ecliptic at accession
─────────
145°31'   Prog. longitude
120°00'   Subtract four signs
─────────
 25°31'♌  Prog. M. C.
```

This of course means the progressed IVth (the father) was
in 25°31'♒, in sextile to Jupiter 25°40' ♐. The disparity of
9' is due to taking the aspect in ecliptic.   It disappears when
we consider that Jupiter was in 0°26'N latitude and that its
sextile in 25°40'♒ in this latitude gives R. A. 327°47' and that
the R. A. of 25°31'♒ on ecliptic (sine latitude) is also 327°47'.
This means the sextile of the IVth to Jupiter is taken in the
latitude of the planet along a parallel plane 0°26'N of the
ecliptic, just as in the preceding calculation the IVth is brought
to the trine of Saturn in Saturn's latitude. Both these planets
are so much more massive than the earth which describes the
ecliptic path that in directing to them **the electromagnetic
coupling is much stronger in their field planes than in that of
the earth.** The Solar sidereal arc never fails to time events
when the error of taking all directions in the ecliptic (without
latitude) is eliminated. However, only the good judgment
which years of experience brings will enable the student to
choose the proper plane for each direction, as it often happens

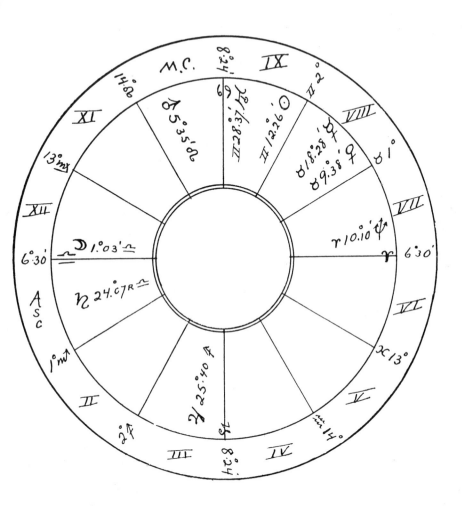

HIS MAJESTY GEORGE V

Birthday Locality at London

the event is such that the direction must be taken to one planet in the plane of another planet's electromagnetic field.

As there may be readers who are none too familiar with the Placidian equation, or who having mastered it still do not fully grasp how the true Solar sidereal arc relates to it, let us see how the arcs of direction, 46°10′ and 42°45′ as used in this case, are obtained. Several different procedures are possible to obtain these arcs, but only two will be cited here.

The death of Edward VII occurred on May 6, 1910. Subtracting from this the birth date, June 3, 1865, we obtain 44 years and 11 months, or in terms of the age arc (Ptolemaic arc) we may express this as 44°55′. Turning to **Raphael's Ephemeris** for 1865 and counting off 44 days from June 3rd, we find that on July 17th the Sun at Greenwich Noon was in 24°50′.5♋. The apparent Sun here moves 57′ a day. So in 55/60 of a day it will move 52′ more, or to 25°42′.5♋. But His Majesty was born 10 hrs. 42 min. **before** noon, and in that time the apparent Sun at the rate of 57′ a day moved 25′.5. As this value is in this case subtractive because the birth time was **before** noon, we have 25°17′♋ as the progressed longtiude of what some would term the "secondary" Sun according to the Placidian rule of terming a solar day as a year of life. From this the two arcs become

Prog. Sun 25°17′♋	115°17′ Long. and	117°14′.5 R. A.
Natal Sun 12°26′♊	72°26′ Long. and	70°57′.5 R. A.
Placidian Arcs	42°51′ Long. Arc	46°17′ R. A. Arc
Reduction	—07′	– -07′
Solar sidereal arc	42°44′ Long.	46°10′ R. A. Arc

The reduction is obtained by allowing one minute for about every six years of age, as earlier mentioned in this chapter.

The arcs may often be found more exactly by the **time** formula as follows:

Time equation for birth	— 10h	42m	
Time equation for event	— 1h	50m	(a)
Time equation sidereal corr.	— 2h	57m	(b)
Total equation in time	— 15h	29m	

And,

Sun's rate	0°57′	log.	1.4025
Equation	15ʰ29′	log.	.1903
	—0°37′	log.	1.5928

Hence,

Longitude Sun on 45th day	25°48′♋	
Correction for time	—0°37′	
True Long. prog. Sun	25°11′♋	117°08′ R. A.
True Long. rad. Sun	12°26′♊	70°58′ R. A.
True arcs	Long. 42°45′	46°10′ R. A.

The corrective (a) is obtained by the expression

$$\frac{28 \times 24 \text{ hrs.}}{365}$$

wherein 28 is the number of days between the event and the 45th birthday. Corrective (b) is obtained by multiplying the age by the time value earlier given, namely 3′56″, the reduction of the Solar-day ephemeris into terms of sidereal days, the latter being the measure of a year of life.

The student should in either of these manners check up all the event arcs used in **Cases 1, 2 and 3** to be sure he understands these equations before attempting to apply the principles of this chapter.

Case 3. The ex-Emperor, William II, born January 27th, 1859, 3:03 P. M., Berlin. Sun 7°10′≈.

29°10′ R. A. Greenwich 1930
—0°54′ Correction to 1859 (71 yrs. × 46″.10)

28°16′ R. A. Greenwich 1859
+ 13°24′ Long. Berlin East

41°40′ R. A. Berlin 1859 = M. C. 14°08′ ♉ ;Asc. 26°31′♌†
309°34′ R. A. 7°10′≈ at birth

(a)   351°14′ R. A. of BL = M. C. 20° 27′♓; Asc. 20°48′♋

and,

44°08′ Long. Berlin M. C. 1859 (14°08′ ♉)
307°10′ Long. Sun 7°10′≈ at birth

(b)   351°18′ Long. BL = M. C. 21°18′♓; Asc. 21°23′♋

For illustration the planets have been placed in the (a) figure, which **except for directional purposes** does not in any case differ more than a very few degrees from (b) equations.

Those who will take the trouble to set up the horary nativity from the above birth data will note that in **this** case the horary angles for the hour almost exactly coincide with the world angles in the BL figures. Consequently, Mars and Neptune are elevated on the zenith in both his personal horoscope and in the world figure here shown for Berlin. War (Mars), chaos (Neptune) and abandonment into exile and seclusion (Neptune) resulted from his Napoleonic dream (Neptune) of conquest (Mars). The comparison is apt not only in view of the parallelism of the outcomes of their careers, **but because Napoleon's horary nativity shows these two planets in conjunction in the Midheaven and elevated a little west of the zenith in his BL figure for Paris.**

As the Sun is in the VIIIth house (heritage), opposite Saturn and trine to the elevated Jupiter, we must here again

---

† **Square to his** Uranus on the European M. C. and square to his Moon on its **Nadir.**

expect to find the directions at accession bring out Jupiter and
Saturn. We find this is indeed so as follows:

> 351°14′ R. A. as per (a)
> 28°57′ Solar sidereal arc in R. A. at accession
> ———————
> 380°11′
> 360°00′ Reject circle
> ———————
> 20°11′ Prog RAMC = 21°48′♈ *
> 90°00′
> ———————
> 110°11′ O. A. in latitude 52°31′ = Asc. 11°41′♌.

This is sextile to Jupiter in 11°41′♊. Proving this arc by
trigonometry we have, as example of the procedure, the following equations:

> 11°41′♌ 41°41′ from ♋ cosine 9.873223
> 23°27′.5 O. E. sine 9.599972
> ————————
> 17°18′ Declination sine 9.473195

and,

> 17°18′ Declination tangent 9.493410
> 52°31′ Lat. Berlin tangent 0.115281
> ————————
> 23°58′ Asc. Diff. sine 9.608691

and,

> 11°41′♌, 41°41′ from ♋ cotangent 0.050392
> 23°27′.5 O. E. cosine 9.962535
> ————————
> 44°09′ R. A. from ♋ cotangent 0.012927
> 90°00′ Add quadrant
> ————————
> 134°09′ R. A. of 11°41′♌, the sextile of Jupiter.
> —23°58′ A. D. in latitude of Berlin, as above
> ————————
> 110°11′ O. A. required, as above obtained by direction.

For the ecliptic equation we have

> 351°18′ Long BL M. C. as per (b)
> 29°37′ Solar sidereal arc in longitude at event.
> ————————
> 380°55′
> 360°00′ Reject circle
> ————————
> 20°55′♈ Long. prog. M. C. = 19°19′ R. A.
> 90°00′
> ————————
> 109°19′ O. A.

This is the oblique ascension required to bring the Ascendant sextile to Jupiter in the latitude of Saturn. For by the
above procedure we obtain

$$11°41' \Omega \text{ in lat. Saturn } 0°47'N = 134°24' \text{ R. A.}$$
$$11°41' \Omega \text{ in lat. Saturn } 0°47'N = \underline{-25°07' \text{ A. D.}}$$
$$109°17' \text{ O. A.}$$

Thus for his accession to the throne we find the Ascendant exactly sextile to Jupiter in the ecliptic plane by the R. A.
arc and the Ascendant within 2' of exact sextile to Jupiter in
the Saturn plane by the ecliptic arc.

Directing the geocentric Ascendant on the R. A. arc it will
be found it was 28°12' Ω at the opening of the Great War,
this being the mean square of the opposition of the Moon to
Uranus† as obtained by the following equation.

$$\frac{\text{Moon } 26°52' + \text{Uranus } 29°34' \, \text{ʊ}}{2} = 28°13' \Omega.$$

These bodies were in the Midheaven and Nadir of the progressed figure. The German breakdown and the flight of the
Emperor to Holland was the final result of Uranus occupying
the Midheaven under this arc.

If we direct the Ascendant on the ecliptic arc of the Sun,
(b) equation, we obtain 28°26' Ω, bringing the same mean-
square aspect to June, 1914, when the assassination of Ferdinand brought the "inducement" (ecliptic arc) to the war in
August. It should here be noted that the great eclipse of
August 21st, 1914, which has been analysed in the preceding
chapter of this work and in the treatise on the fixed stars,
occurred in close conjunction with the progressed Ascendant,

---

* A seven-hour angle (105°) from his progressed Saturn in 6°48' Ω, at that
time. This electrical axis is found in felspar. It has been repeatedly found to
be a powerful aspect for calamity.

† These planets being respectively trine and sextile to Mars in the Midheaven.
The sidereal arc is 52°59', and if this is taken from the BL R. A. 351°14', it
brings the M. C. converse to 26°14' ♑, in close sextile to his Mars and Moon.

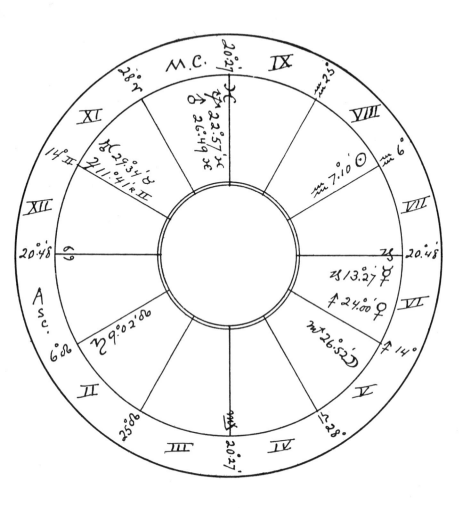

WILLIAM II

Birthday Localtiy at Berlin

and conjunction with the progressed M. C. of the London BL figure for George V.

It is interesting to note that if we further examine what Professor Jeans in defining the Einstein view terms "a tangle of world lines," we find that England's support of France in this war, to the great detriment of the German cause, is shown by **the Emperor's progressed BL Midheaven at Paris in square to Mars in the horoscope and BL figure of King George.** The equation follows:

$$28°16'\ \text{R. A. Greenwich in 1859 (the Emperor's epoch)}$$
$$\underline{+2°20'}\ \text{Longitude of Paris East}$$
$$30°36'\ \text{R. A. of Paris in 1859}$$
$$\underline{309°34'}\ \text{R. A. Emperor's Sun } 7°10'\text{♒ at birth.}$$
$$340°10'\ \text{R. A. BL M. C. at Paris}$$
$$\underline{52°59'}\ \text{Solar sidereal arc in R. A. at opening of the war}$$
$$393°09'$$
$$360°00'\ \text{Reject circle}$$
$$\underline{33°09'}\ \text{R. A. prog. BL } = \text{ M. C. } 5°27'\text{♉.}$$

This is square to King George's Mars in 5°30'♌. Five minutes is here taken from the place of Mars to reduce it to the zodiac of the Emperor's birth, the equivalent of ecliptic precession in the interval from 1865 to 1859. If we calculate the above cross direction by the **ecliptic arc,** we obtain in this instance exactly the same result, showing the "inducements" (ecliptic arc) for England taking up the sword against Germany in support of France did not arise till the "current of events" (R. A. arc) and the "cause of right" (right ascensional arc) **at the same time** made it imperative. Thus to the "last moment" (coincident arcs in both planes) Germany could not believe England would interfere. It is well known square aspects signify interference.

This example may help the reader to grasp the fact earlier emphasized. Namely, that the arcs in the ecliptic plane time the voltage induction due to the magnetic field which is perpendicular to the electric field as defined by the ecliptic plane†, and that the arcs in the right ascensional plane time the earth or armature rotation across the magnetic field and define the "commutative moments" of objective current flow, or the "current events" in the world.   In the above example there was no "lag" or "lead", as the electrician would say, in the setting of the commutator brushes with respect to the line of the pole pieces.   With scarcely a warning spark at the point of friction or commutation, the cosmic generator plunged England and Germany into war for and against France within the space of a day or two as July, as one ashamed, bade August com-plete the stage for the shambles.

Lest the reader conclude that these three cases were among the reasons for adopting the precessional base from which Table I is computed, the author is in position to prove none of these cases were computed until this work was being compiled, long after the base had been established by hundreds of other tests. Indeed, at the time it was established by **theory and by histori-cal events** that the Greenwich meridian on the precessional dial co-ordinates R. A. 29°10′ in 1930, **it was not even known the BL figures could be directed on the Solar arc with such mathe-matical timing of events concerning the relation of the human equation to the community or national life.**   Can there be better citations to convince the reader that the use of the table will satisfy his tests in this field of its application no less than in his study of eclipses with reference to world events?

To what degree of accuracy the BL figure may be directed for events which have apparently less and less bearing on the community or national life, is a matter for future investigation. Theoretically no personal event can be without its influence, directly or indirectly, upon the Cosmic Body; but practically speaking its reaction may not always be at the place where we may be inclined to seek for it.   Thus a man through sick-

† See Figs. 5, 6, 7, **The Stars, How and Where They Influence.**

ness may lose a position in the town of D and as a result may move to E and become influential in its official life, and so the arc of sickness may register stronger at the latter place, provided his position at D was of purely private import, or provided it was filled by a man from F who by temperament and training was so much the same as to make the change in the human equation of no moment to the town D. But if the successor from F was therein of considerable community standing and left there solely because the vacancy at D called him, then it is probable the other individual's sickness would register in his BL figure at F; since under all these circumstances it would affect the Cosmic Body more at F than at D. Or the major consequences may even be thus "relayed" through a number of places. Great oaks from little acorns grow. The chain of cause and effect is an unbroken series that may be amplified or diminished at each point of transformation according to the degree and phase of electromagnetic coupling at each stage.

This will perhaps be clear only to those who have made a thorough digest of such works as Morecroft's **Principles of Radio Communication**, than which there is no better groundwork for those who wish to enlarge their grasp of the uses of this text. It is recognized as an authorative reference for those who would approach the Invisible Power through the door of science—if such it be the reader has not found understanding and comfort before the altar of exhortation. Faith is both essential and magnificent. Of itself it offers no understanding. Over their diverse means to the unified end of faith **plus** understanding only fools will quarrel.

Case 4. John J. Astor, born July 13th, 1864. Hour unknown. He sank with the Titanic on April 14th, 1912, in longitude 50°15′ West, latitude 41°16′ North. This case is cited to show, as nearly as possible, the equations in **longitude,**

because in the author's text on the fixed stars it is shown how they defined the fatal **latitude.**

No **exact** BL or progressed equations can be shown because in this case the hour of birth is unknown and consequently the Sun's longitude and the BL zeniths at birth are uncertain **by some part of one degree.** The directional arcs will not be significantly in error, because no matter what the hour may be it effects nearly equally the positons of the natal and progressed Sun's positions whose **difference** is the arc of direction. But because these directional arcs apply to the BL zeniths and these are subject to a fractional degree of error, so the progressed angles will be uncertain by a like amount. It is often possible to use the BL calculations to determine the true longitude of the Sun and from this determine the birth hour; but as such a procedure belongs to the art of rectifying nativities it is entirely outside the scope of the present text.

Solving for the place, we have:

29°10′ R. A. Greenwich 1930
—0°51′ Correction to 1864 (66 yrs. × 46″.10)
28°19′ R. A. 1864. (Add the circle to subtract)
—50°15′ Longitude of event West
338°04′ R. A. of place = M. C. 6°18′ ♓.

This is sesquiquadrate to his Sun in about 21° ♋, over which Neptune was transiting at the time; also trine to the Moon, which was in oppositon to Mars and excited by the transit of Uranus and by stars No. 262 and 538 circling in the fatal latitude.

For the BL figure, we have, approximately:

338°04′
112°48′ R. A. Sun at Greenwich noon on birthday
(a)   90°52′ RAMC   =   M. C. 0°48′ ♋; Asc. 0°41′ ♎

and,

336°18′   Long. of place in ecliptic (6°18′ ♓)
111°06′   Long. Sun at Greenwich noon on birthday
───────
447°24′
420°00′   Reject 14 even signs.

(b)   27°24′ ♊ M. C.

As at birth Uranus was in 26°52′ ♊ and at death had progressed to 29°00′ ♊, we see it was respectively close to the BL
zeniths. Its role in sudden catastrophies is familiar to all astrological observers. Mars was transiting the place of Uranus on
the date of the tragedy, and the text on the fixed stars shows
No. 1463 of Boss' Catalogue was in R. A. conjunction with
these points and circling in 41°21′ south latitude, nadir to the
fatal latitude as shown in that text.

Directing, we have approximately:

90°52′   R. A. of BL as per (a)
45°35′   Solar sidereal arc in R. A. at death
───────
136°27′   Prog. R. A. = M. C. 13°59′ ♌, which is the semi-
          square of progressed Uranus in 29°00′ ♊.

and,

87°24′   Long. of BL as per (b)
45°32′   Solar sidereal arc in ecliptic at death.
───────
132°56′
120°00′   Sub. four signs.

12°56′ ♌ which is the mean semisquare of natal and pro-
          gressed Uranus.

If we direct the Ascendants of these figures we find about
5° to 6° ♏ rising. **This would be conjunction with the Moon
(if the hour of birth was A. M.)** in its opposition to Mars,
which latter was conjunction with stars No. 262 and No. 538
(Boss Catalogue), circling respectively in **the latitude of the
collision and the sinking,** as shown in the companion text on
the fixed stars†.

───────────────────────

† See Chapter V, **Case 1, The Stars, How and Where They Influence.**

Mrs. Astor, who was saved from the wreck and inherited a large fortune, was born June 19th, 1891. Her Jupiter in 17°♓ was in the locality Midheaven and the Sun directed trine to Jupiter in the fatal year. Her BL figure at the place shows Mercury, Venus and Neptune at the zenith, and the directed Midheaven was conjunction with her Sun.

Vincent Astor, born November 15th, 1891, inherited some sixty-five millions following his father's tragic death. His Jupiter was 8° Pisces, on the locality zenith of the fatal longitude. His BL zenith there was conjunction with Uranus, which was in benefic trine to Jupiter and as in Mrs. Astor's case his progressed BL Midheaven was at the time conjunction with his Sun in that longitude.

John J. Astor, Jr., was born four months after the tragedy, on August 14th, 1912. Venus and Mercury were conjunction with the Nadir of the locality, in square to Jupiter. Jupiter was just rising in the BL figure there .

These last two citations show how a locality may signify fortune to some members of a family and tragedy to another, even though the beneficiary resides at a distant point, or, as in the latter case, was as yet unborn. The latter is another striking proof that time is not what man assumes it to be. It is, as dreams also tend to prove, one of the variable illusions arising out of the nature of consciousness as itself a variable depending on the different frequency constants of the planets, each of which while reflecting a minimum of the solar waves at light frequencies, for the greater part reflect to earth a different note thereof, quite invisible but capable of so altering our timesense as to render all our work-a-day notions of time and space purely relative*. It is thus Einstein has the materialistic army of scientists by the ears.

We must not forget that there are but seven planets re-

* See Chapter XI, The Stars, How and Where They Influence.

flecting the Solar waves to us on earth, and try as he will man's ingenuity has never succeeded in inventing a musical instrument that will give out more than seven fundamental notes. **The masses and diameters of the planets determine their oscillatory frequencies as certainly as the same factors determine the frequency constant of a radio transmitter's crystal control.** Each planet reflects **many harmonics** but only **one note.**

In this connection perhaps a few readers may recall a recent editorial by a brilliant columnist who, writing on the predisposition of man to fumble in his thinking, cites Kepler as a man of genius in formulating the planetary law which bears his name, and as a fumbler who spent years trying to decide which musical note was ruled by each planet. Was Kepler fumbling when he did this, or is our entertaining columnist fumbling when he thinks Kepler was a genius in the one instance and so foolish in the other? Let present and future radio facts answer.

In concluding the Titanic picture it may be noted that William Stead, who went down in this disaster, was born July 5th, 1849. Among the configurations **was the progressed BL Ascendant in approximate opposition to his Mars,** which as shown in the companion text was conjunction with stars No. 262 and No. 538 coupled with the fatal **latitudes** via the stars' radial fields as mentioned with reference to Astor.

Case 5. Charles Post, Born October 26th, 1854. Suicide at Santa Barbara, California, May 9th, 1914. A brief reference to this case is illuminating as the **latitudinal** equation is given in the companion text. In this case the hour is unknown, as in the above citations, and nothing would be gained in presenting the actual calculations. The student, however, should check up the following statements to the nearest round degrees possible.

The BL Midheaven was very close sesquiquadrate to his Mars, which was conjunction with star No. 4258, daily circl-ing over the exact latitude of Santa Barbara at the epoch of his birth.   See Chapter V, Case 4, of the other text.   The progressed BL Ascendant was opposite Saturn and near Mars in their mutual opposition and square to Neptune.   The pro-gressed Ascendant was also quincunx with Uranus, which was conjunction with star No. 646 circling in that latitude. Uranus indicates the nature of the death, Mars the means to the end (a shotgun), and Saturn (chronic ill health) supplied the motive.

Case 6.   Henry Ford, July 30th, 1863.

In this case the Moon held the locality zenith at Detroit, and in his early manhood the town was quite convinced he was a lunar subject who though harmless could come to no good. Time of course proved the town's notion of him, not Ford, was crazy. Uranus, lord of automotives, was rising in the Detroit locality—and so was Ford, though possibly he himself did not early know it.   In the BL figure Uranus was about 8° east of the zenith and in trine to Jupiter in the IInd house (wealth). Thus his tremendous success (zenith) in invention and auto manufacturing (Uranus), and wealth (Jove in the IInd) thrown in for good measure.   Directing the BL figure for 1903 when the Ford Company was launched, we find Jupiter was then conjunction with the Ascendant—always the best symbol for successful financing; though this ray found its medium in the person of James Couzens without whose timely interest Ford history would hardly be quite the same.   For Ford in those days was still the inventor, not the man of finance he has since become.   The point, however, is this: When and where a given result is staged, the human mediums necessary to that end always appear, as certainly as a flood where the eclipse sets the storm's path.

Case 7. Thomas Edison, February 11, 1847, about 11:30 P. M.

In this case, as in that of Ford and so many exceptionally successful inventors, Jupiter was in benefic aspect to Uranus. Let us see how this was brought out in and about Orange, N. J., the position of which is 40°46′N and 74°13′W. In the nativity Jupiter was 6°53′Ⅱ, in sextile to Uranus in 11°34′♈.

Solving for the place, we have:

29°10′ RAMC Greenwich in 1900, Table I
—1°04′ Correctoin to 1847 (83 yrs. × 46″.10)
———————
28°06′ RAMC Greenwich in 1847
360°00′ Add circle to subtract longtiude
———————
388°06′
—74°13′ Longitude of Orange west
———————
313°53′ R. A. = M. C. Orange 11°25′♒, sextile Uranus 11°34′♈.

Taking the arc on the ecliptic results in an error of 9′, or about as many miles. But his Uranus was in 0°39′S and his Jupiter and Neptune respectively in 0°31′S and 0°32′S. His horary Midheaven was about 12°♌, in trine to Uranus. Hence we should couple the locality **Nadir** trine to Uranus in the field planes of these planets. For that of Jupiter and Neptune, we have:

133°53′ R. A. 11°34′♌ (trine Uranus) in lat. Jupiter 0°31′S
180°
———————
313°53′ RAMC of locality as above computed.

Taking the coupling in the field of Uranus brings it about two miles farther east, or about East Orange.

For the locality Ascendant, we have:

313°53′ RAMC Orange for 1847, as above
90°00′
———————
403°53′
360°00′
———————
43°53′ O. A.

This O. A. in latitude 40°46′N gives the Orange Ascend⁓
ant as 5°22′♊ at that epoch. This is near his Jupiter in
6°53′♊, the **present** Ascendant for that point being about
6°40′♊. Here it may be said that if the student will compute
the locality Descendant opposite Jupiter in the field planes of
Edison's Venus and Saturn, 1°29′S, he will find the coupling
centers at Menlo Park.

Now the BL couplings:

```
313°53′ RAMC Orange, for Ingress 1847
325°15′ R. A. Edison's Sun in 22°54′.♒
─────
639°08′
360°00′ Reject circle
─────
279°08′ R. A. BL  =  M. C. 8°23′♑.
```

This is conjunction with his Moon in 7°38′♑ and sextile to
Venus. The Moon being in mundo (R. A.) conjunction with
America's foremost star, Vega, circling over Washington.

And for the BL Ascendant:

```
279°08′ RAMC as above
 90°00′
─────
369°08′
360°00′ Reject circle
─────
  9°08′ O. A., which in latitude 40°46′N gives the ecliptic
       Ascendant of Orange as 15°45′♈.
```

As this is over 4° east of Edison's Uranus in 11°34′♈, the
beginner will wonder why the "electrical wizard" (Uranus)
did not choose a little more western place for his experiments
(Uranus). But from all reports it has been Edison's role to
furnish the **ideas** (Mercury) and leave most of their trial and
experimentation (Uranus) to his aids. **Therefore we should
couple the BL Ascendant with Uranus in the electric field of
Mercury.** Testing this we find:

```
Uranus 11°34′♈ in lat. Mercury 2°05′S  = R. A. 11°26′
Uranus 11°34′♈ in lat. Mercury 2°05′S  = Dec.  2°40′
```

and,

Declination	2°40′	tangent	8.668160
Latitude	40°46′	tangent	9.935589
A. D.	2°18′	sine	8.603749

and,

R. A.	11°26′
A. D.	—2°18′
O. A.	9°08′, which is the O. A. of the BL Ascendant as above computed.

This coupling is shown in Fig. 5, wherein it is also shown that star No. 175, circling geographic latitudes from 40°34′N in 1847 to 40°53′N at the present epoch, was in R. A. 10°21′ in his birth year and coupled with his Uranus. Thus defining the latitude of the electrical wizard's (Uranus) main activities. In Fig. 5 the coupling of the star and Uranus is shown in the main drawing in 0°39′N, whereas Uranus was in 0°39′S. This is merely a convenient way of representing the planet's and star's 180° phase coupling at D in the "tangle of world lines."

For:

190°22′ R. A. 11°34′≏ (opp. Uranus) in Uranus' lat. 0°39′S
—180°
10°22′ The R. A. of star No. 175.

That is, Uranus' opposition in its own field plane intersected the star's lower meridian. If such calculations prove a little difficult to understand, the beginner should lay aside his astrological texts and take a brief course in electromagnetism. Once he understands the principles of magnetic induction and phase couplings as they apply to alternating current practice at all frequencies from those of a low-cycle dynamo to those of the light spectrum, he will experience far less difficulty in reasoning out the necessary calculations for the particular problem; particularly if he will keep in mind that the electric and mag-

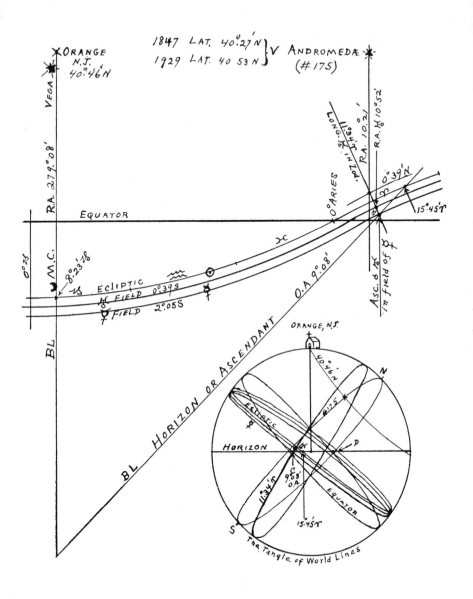

FIG 5

145

netic fields of a wave are always perpendicular to each other
no matter how many other waves they may intersect or hetero-
dyne with.   The planes of the induced fields are then determined from combining these vectorially.*

Case 8.   John D. Rockefeller, July 8th, 1839.

In this case Neptune, King of Oil, was on the zenith of the
New York meridian and elevated in all figures of the Eastern
and Middle States.   The Moon, the illuminator, was rising in
the Ascendant.   In the BL figure at Titusville, Pa., where oil
was first struck on August 27th, 1859, his Venus was just
rising, and this figure directed to his 20th year brings the
Moon to the zenith.   Thus began the story of oil as an illumi-
nant.   Of course the zenith was then also square to Uranus
(the drill) which was then on the **descendant,** going down to
the "strike" (Uranus).

Case 9.   Woodrow Wilson, December 28th, 1856.
Here the computer will find Venus and Mars, the lords
of peace and war, closely joined on the Midheaven of Eastern
America.   And so for nearly three years this idealist kept the
nation out of the war, even voyaged to Europe in the cause of
peace, only to see the red god triumph and cast his dragnet
westward across the Atlantic to our western shores.   In his
BL figure for Washington, Uranus, the dictator, was at the
nadir—down, down, far down, for the Potsdam Czar; but
down, too, for Wilson in the role of **individualist.**   In this figure Venus and Mars were rising, first Venus (peace) then
Mars (war).   Directing the figure to 1917, when America
entered the war, brings the XIth angle (friends, **allies) in**
conjunction with Venus and Mars.   Thus the die was cast
for the Allied Forces.

---

*   See Morecroft's **Principles of Radio Communication,** pages 8 and 318.

Case 10. George Washington, February 22nd, 1732.

In this case we find the Washington Midheaven of the epoch to be 7°13′≈, conjunction with his Mercury in 7°15′≈, in close trine to Jupiter and sextile to Uranus. Thus arose the tale of the cherry tree (Mercury), the keen sense of justice (Jupiter) and the connection with the revolutionary (Uranus) cause. The BL figure shows his Moon at the zenith and in conjunction with the bright star Vega, which, circling over the latitude of Washington the past few hundred years, is one of the several star significators of our federal government. Vega is one of the brightest stars and the largest in Lyra, that eagle-like bird that strums the harp—watchful, but disposed to make harmony. If we direct the BL figure on the R. A. arc to the 4th of July, 1776, we find the zenith then 23°08′≈, square to his Mars in 23°11 ♏. Here again the war indication is clear.

Case 11. Abraham Lincoln, February 12th, 1809.

Here we find the Washington Midheaven in 8°12′≈, in sextile to his Venus, but square to Uranus—the man of peace (Venus) involved in revolution (Uranus). The BL figures show 6°♑ on the zenith, this being near the right ascension of Vega, the square of his Venus and the sextile of his Uranus. As in Washington's case the Moon was elevated in the Midheaven of the BL figure. The elevation of the moon shows the part plain common sense played in their administrations of their high office and their contributions to the cause of the plain people, who in all figures are symbolized by the Moon. Directing the BL figure brings the Midheaven conjunction with the Sun with his rise to the presidency and trine to Mars during the Civil War*.

---

* Compare with Case 13, in which we find the M. C. conjunction Mars early in the World War and conjunction Sun at Hoover's rise to the presidency.

Case 12. Calvin Coolidge, July 4th, 1872.

Here the student will find the only really high planet in the Washington precessional figure was Saturn in the IXth house, in zodiacal conjunction with Vega. Consequently, the **overtone** of his administration can be summed up in such Saturn synonyms as duty, labor, economy and silence. In the BL figure, however, 27°36′ ♉ is on the zenith, placing the Moon, Mars, Venus, Sun, Mercury and Jupiter all high in the XIth house (friends, assistance, **succession**). Directing, we will see that the zenith passed Mars years before he attained to office; therefore it had no war significance during his administration. The Midheaven passed Venus about the close of the Great War and his rise to Governor of Massachusetts. There followed the BL Midheaven over the Sun and his election as Vice President, and with the sweep of the Washington meridian over the oppositon of Saturn, natal and progressed, came the passing of Harding, the onus of the presidency and the passing of Calvin Junior, which has wrung from this intensely humane (Sun joined with Venus) though cryptic (Sun opposite Saturn) soul the succinct phrase, "It costs a lot to be President."

Case 13. President Hoover, August 10th, 1874.

For this date we find Saturn 10°29′♒, close to the Washington zenith in 9°01′♒ at his epoch and near which his progressed Saturn will come "stationary" in 7°40′♒ in the next few years. From this it may be said that those who foresee he cannot maintain or even surpass the Coolidge economic (Saturn) program are doomed to change their thinking. More than in any other President here is the Saturnian archenemy of waste (Neptune), the overtone of the strict utilitarian (Saturn), the stabilizer (Saturn) of business and government (M. C.), the man to promote the success (M. C.) of the farmer (Saturn) if that be possible, the man to whose past record (Saturn) the nation may perpetually turn for the measure

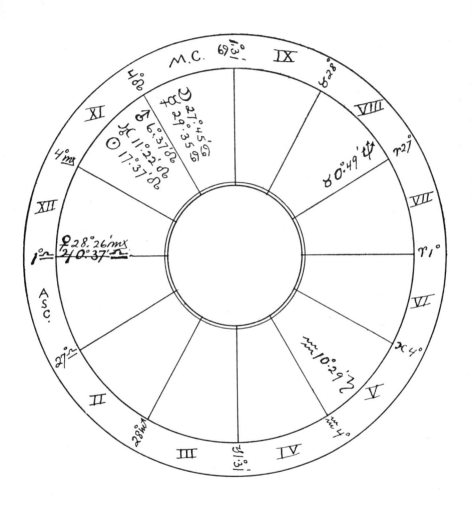

HERBERT HOOVER

Birthday Locality at Washington

of its success (M. C.) under his administration, and for that settling down (Saturn) process which for the first time in the history of the nation marks the crucial bend in the road to sobriety and a settled maturity.   What America **has** accomplished has been the accomplishment of youth's spontaneity and venturesomely creative optimism, with all its attendant waste. What it is about to learn, more than in the Coolidge regime, is the need of conservation and security (Saturn) of the place it has attained, the measure of its limitations and the remembrance that while it still has a future (Neptune) of great engineering (Uranus) possibilities it has by now accumulated a **past** (Saturn) to profit by and a debt to pay to it.

In the accompanying BL figure we see the Moon and Mercury well elevated toward the zenith and in benefic sextile to Venus and Jupiter just rising, while Mars, Uranus and the Sun hold the XIth house. A splendid figure†. Directing it we find the zenith passed Mars during the early period of the war, moved on to the opposition of Saturn when as Food Controller he drew the ire of the farmers (Saturn), but with the zenith over Uranus displayed the characteristic Uranian engineering efficiency as dictator in that capacity and in the reorganization of the Department of Commerce relative in particular to the extension of American commerce abroad— wider and wider **distribution** of the industrial fruits of invention being one of the foremost expressions of **Uranus'** note from the cosmic harp. With 1928 the zenith directed to the Sun and with it came his nomination for and election to the central office of the nation. With the inauguration, and the passing of the Ascendant square to Uranus, came the Mexican revolution and the extension of his characteristic engineering skill to the big job.   The proximate square of the Ascendant to

† Though readers will note that the five most elevated bodies in the figure have now all passed the zenith, and that the rising Venus and Jupiter cannot reach the Eastern M. C. during his lifetime.

Saturn sounding its first dry note with the prompt passing of the Jones Bill. In the opposition of the Sun and Uranus to Saturn, however, may be seen much opposition to his policies.

To close this work with citations showing how this text may be used in a comprehensive study of leading figures in any particular field of endeavor, let us now turn to a few celebrities of the American stage. It is hardly necessary to state that Venus is the principal significator in this respect. Briefing the BL features we find as follows, for New York.

George Cohan	Venus 4° east of zenith, trine to Jupiter
J. T. Powers	Venus 2° east of the zenith
Lew Fields	Venus and Mercury conjunction on zenith
Forbes-Robertson	Venus, Mercury and Jupiter on the zenith
David Warfield	Venus with Mercury rising trine to Moon
Billie Burke	Venus with Saturn on the midheaven
Ada Rehan	Venus with Neptune on the midheaven
Lillian Russell	Venus on the midheaven sextile Jupiter
Madam Melba	Venus with Mercury on the midheaven
Viola Allen	Venus with Saturn rising square to zenith

The list could be indefinitely extended, but these suffice to point the way.

When the birth hour is known the horary nativity is not to be ignored, but all these examples give some hint of what may be done without it, and of the vital part the world stage, as defined by this text, plays in every career, and the relations of opportunity to such good or indifferent talents as the individual may possess.

A good peg is a good peg, but it must find the hole it fits.

—THE END—